INSIGHT GUIDES

ORLANDO
StepbyStep

APA PUBLICATIONS L
Part of the Langenscheidt Publishing Group

CONTENTS

Above from top: the Tampa Bay Rays of St Petersburg; the flora in Florida; catching some rays; stunning peacock; taking the boat out on the emerald green Florida waters.

ABOUT THIS BOOK

This *Step by Step Guide* has been produced by the editors of Insight Guides, whose books have set the standard for visual travel guides since 1970. With top-quality photography and authoritative recommendations, this guidebook brings you the very best of Orlando in a series of 15 tailor-made tours.

WALKS AND TOURS

The tours in the book provide something to suit all budgets, tastes and trip lengths. As well as covering Orlando's many classic attractions – notably its parks – the routes also track lesser-known sights and up-and-coming areas; there are also excursions for those who want to extend their visit outside the city center. The tours embrace a range of interests, so whether you are an animal lover, an art fan, a daredevil, a Disney aficionado or have kids to entertain, you will find an option to suit.

We recommend that you read the whole of a tour before setting out. This should help you to familiarize yourself with the route and enable you to plan where to stop for refreshments –

options for this are shown in the 'Food and Drink' boxes, recognizable by the knife and fork sign, on most pages.

For our pick of the walks by theme, consult Recommended Tours For… *(see pp.6–7).*

OVERVIEW

The tours are set in context by this introductory section, giving an overview of the city and a summary of its parks to set the scene, plus background information on food and drink and shopping. A succinct history timeline in this chapter highlights the key events that have shaped Orlando over the centuries.

DIRECTORY

Also supporting the tours is a Directory chapter, comprising a user-friendly, clearly organized A–Z of practical information, our pick of where to stay while you are in the city and select restaurant listings; these eateries complement the more low-key cafés and restaurants that feature within the tours themselves and are intended to offer a wider choice for evening dining.

The Author

Donna Dailey is a travel writer and photographer whose work appears in magazines and newspapers worldwide. Her articles have won several prestigious travel writing awards. She has written a great number of travel guidebooks to destinations in Europe, Africa and America, including guides to Dublin and Denver for Insight and Berlitz Los Angeles. Her fascination with Florida began with childhood visits to the theme parks and beaches, but for her the star attraction is the amazing wildlife and sea life that thrives here, even in the heart of Orlando.

Margin Tips
Shopping tips, historical facts, handy hints and information on activities help visitors to make the most of their time in Orlando.

Feature Boxes
Notable topics are highlighted in these special boxes.

Key Facts Box
This box gives details of the distance covered on the tour, plus an estimate of how long it should take. It also states where the route starts and finishes, and gives key travel information such as which days are best to do the route or handy transport tips.

Footers
Look here for the tour name, a map reference and the main attraction on the double page.

Food and Drink
Recommendations of where to stop for refreshment are given in these boxes. The numbers prior to each restaurant/café name link to references in the main text. On city maps, restaurants are plotted. Note that not all park restaurants have telephone numbers, but we have included details for those those that do.

The $ signs at the end of each entry reflect the approximate cost of a two-course meal for one, with half a bottle of house wine, not including tax and tip. These should be seen as a guide only. Price ranges, also quoted on the inside back flap for easy reference, are:

$$$ US$50 and above
$$ US$25–50
$ US$25 and below

Route Map
Detailed cartography shows the itinerary clearly plotted with numbered dots. For more detailed mapping, see the pull-out map slotted inside the back cover.

ANIMAL LOVERS

Swim with the dolphins at Discover Cover (tour 7) and let magnificent killer whales and other marine creatures entertain you at SeaWorld (tour 7). See exotic animals along jungle trails at Disney's Animal Kingdom (tour 4) and go on a Serengeti Safari at Busch Gardens Africa (tour 15).

RECOMMENDED TOURS FOR...

ART BUFFS

Browse the art galleries in Downtown Orlando (tour 8), visit the Mennello Museum and Orlando Museum of Art in Loch Haven Park (tour 9), the Morse Museum in Winter Park (tour 12), and the Salvadore Dalí Museum in Tampa Bay (tour 15).

CHILDREN

Step into storybook worlds at the Magic Kingdom's Fantasyland (tour 1) or Islands of Adventure's Seuss Landing (tour 6). Dinosaurs, robots and hands-on fun await at the Orlando Science Center (tour 9).

ESCAPING THE CROWDS

Go beachcombing on the sandy stretches of Cocoa Beach (route 14) or Fort De Soto Park (route 15). Explore the trails at Wekiwa Springs, Blue Springs State Park or Merritt Island (routes 13 and 14).

FOODIES

Munch your way around the world at Epcot's World Showcase (tour 2). Visit some of the city's best restaurants in Downtown Orlando (tour 8) and Winter Park (tour 12), or head for Tampa (tour 15) where Bern's Steak House has the world's biggest wine cellar.

HISTORY BUFFS

The Orange County Regional History Center (tour 8) gives a fascinating insight into Central Florida before the theme parks. Explore the history of the space race at the Kennedy Space Center (tour 14), or step back a century into Tampa's Latin Quarter in Ybor City (tour 15).

MOVIE LOVERS

Put yourself in the middle of a tornado at Universal Studios (tour 5) and watch stunt show action at Disney Hollywood Studios (tour 3).

NATURE LOVERS

Take an airboat ride on Lake Toho (tour 11), see manatees in the wild at Blue Springs State Park (tour 13), go canoeing on the Hillsborough River or Wekiwa Springs (tours 15 and 13) or spot wildlife at Merritt Island National Refuge (tour 14).

PARKS AND GARDENS

Stroll along the camellia-lined paths and expansive grounds of the Harry P. Leu Gardens (tour 9), or through the whimsical topiaries and botanical gardens at Cypress Gardens (tour 11).

SHOPPERS

International Drive (tour 10) is a shopper's gateway to flea markets, designer outlet centers and mega-malls. Go bargain hunting along Highway 192 in Kissimmee (tour 11) or escape the chains on Park Avenue in Winter Park (tour 12).

OVERVIEW

An overview of Orlando's geography, development, culture, parks and attractions, plus illuminating background information on food and drink, shopping and history.

CITY INTRODUCTION

With seven major theme parks, several water parks, a myriad cultural and other attractions and the second-largest convention center in the country, Orlando is a huge tourist destination, attracting 48 million visitors a year.

Play Days
Orlando has more than 100 visitor attractions. It would take you about 70 eight-hour days to visit every one. There are 176 public and semi-private golf courses in the metro region, offering more than 545 miles (875 kilometres) of golf.

The city of Orlando lies at the heart of Central Florida's largest metropolitan region. Although it measures only 65 square miles (168 sq km) in Orange County, Greater Orlando covers 2.6 million acres (1.04 million hectares) in adjoining Osceola, Seminole and Lake counties. It encompasses the cities of Kissimmee to the south, Winter Park and Maitland to the north and, to the southwest, Walt Disney World Resort, practically a city in itself. However, there's much more to Orlando than the theme parks that made it famous, from art and cultural offerings to its wildlife and lush environment.

LAKES AND RIVERS

Orlando's landscape is largely flat, and as the city expanded much of the terrain was drained from the natural swamps and wetlands. There are more than 2000 lakes, rivers and springs in Greater Orlando. Shingle Creek, Boggy Creek and other channels form part of a vast watershed that runs all the way to the Everglades.

Dozens of lakes are dotted throughout the urban areas, from Lake Eola in downtown Orlando, to big Lake Toho in Kissimmee, to tiny Lake Lily in Maitland to Winter Park's chain of lakes connected by scenic canals. Wildlife is perfectly at home in this urban environment, and you'll regularly see heron, egrets, storks, wildfowl, turtles and even alligators.

CITY LAYOUT

Downtown Orlando, the city's commercial center, lies several miles north of the theme parks and Convention

Right: Florida is known the world over for its citrus crops.

Center. Interstate 4 (I-4) is the main thoroughfare that links the various parts. It stretches from Tampa Bay on the Gulf Coast northeast through Orlando to Daytona Beach. Highway 528, a toll road also known as the Beachline Expressway, runs from Orlando International Airport west to I-4 and east to Cocoa Beach. International Drive wiggles its way alongside a central stretch of I-4, serving the Convention Center as well as many attractions. Highway 192 in Kissimmee, with its proximity to Disney World, is another major tourist thoroughfare.

RURAL ROOTS

Long before Walt Disney arrived and changed the face of Orlando forever, this was cattle and citrus country. From 1920 to 1954, Dr Philip P. Phillips was the world's largest citrus-grower, with more than 5,000 acres (2,000 hectares) of groves in Orange County. He introduced crop-dusting by plane, and perfected a way to make canned orange juice taste good.

It may be hard to find an orange tree – let alone a grove – in the city today, but special events pay homage to Orlando's rural roots. More than 100,000 oranges, grapefruits and tangerines adorn colorful floats that wind through downtown during the annual Orlando Citrus Parade, held at the end of December. The Silver Spurs Rodeo, which takes place twice a year in Kissimmee, is the largest professional rodeo east of the Mississippi.

PEOPLE

Orlando is a young city. Of the nearly 2 million people who live in the metropolitan region, the median age is just 36. People relocate here from all over the country, and it's estimated that over 1,500 new residents arrive every week.

Disney is of course the top employer, but there are also around 3,000 high-tech companies and major industries including digital media, aviation, aerospace, and biomedicine. Over 150 international firms also have branches here. And with 48,000 students, the University of Central Florida in Orlando is one of America's largest universities.

'Tin Can Tourists'

Central Florida's tourism boom actually started long before Disney. In the 1920s, paved roads and Model-T Fords opened up the region's natural attractions to 'tin can tourists'. They drove south on the Dixie Highway, their cars rigged up with folding side tents, to enjoy the weather and such early attractions as alligator wrestling at Gatorland and dancing mermaids at Weeki Wachee Springs. Their name referred to the cars and the food they ate from tinned cans – they were notorious for their frugality. Governor Fuller Warren said of them: 'They came to Florida with one suit of underwear and one $20 bill, and changed neither.'

Above from far left: Downtown Tampa skyline; Orlando smile; kids watching their Tampa Bay baseball heroes; jai alai is a popular sport in Florida.

Above: Minnie and her friends will always greet you with a smile.

Below: Disney's iconic castle dominates the Magic Kingdom.

THEME PARKS AND ATTRACTIONS

Walt Disney World Resort

Walt Disney World Resort is actually located outside the city limits of Orlando, in the cities of Lake Buena Vista and Bay Lake. Covering more than 25,000 acres (101 sq km), it is made up of four theme parks (the Magic Kingdom, Epcot, Animal Kingdom and Disney Hollywood Studios), two water parks (Typhoon Lagoon and Blizzard Beach), the Downtown Disney dining and shopping district, the Pleasure Island nightlife district, DisneyQuest indoor interactive theme park, Disney's Wide World of Sports complex, other sports

facilities from golf courses to stock car racing, 33 resort hotels, two spas and even a campground. It really is a world in itself.

DisneyQuest

Just because you've visited all four theme parks, you haven't quite 'done Disney World'. There's one more indoor theme park: DisneyQuest. Located in Downtown Disney, it features no less than five floors of high-tech, interactive games and rides. Among the highlights is Pirates of the Caribbean, where you take to the high seas to bag some booty, firing cannonballs and fending off attackers in an amazing pirate ship simulator. Or try the space-age bumper cars in Buzz Lightyear's AstroBlaster. You can even design your own roller coaster on CyberSpace Mountain.

DisneyQuest (open daily 11.30am–11pm, until midnight Fri–Sat; charge) can be visited separately or as part of a resort package.

Downtown Disney

Spread along a lake shore and covering 120 acres (50 hectares), Downtown Disney consists of three parts. West Side focuses on dining and entertainment, with cinemas, Cirque du Soleil's La Nouba, House of Blues and restaurants such as Planet Hollywood and Bongos Cuban Café. Pleasure Island is the nightlife area with a variety of bars and nightclubs. Marketplace is geared for shopping and also has several restaurants. There is no admission fee to the complex; hours vary by location.

Universal Orlando Resort

Universal Orlando Resort is located in central Orlando between the Convention Center and downtown. It comprises two theme parks – Universal Studios Florida and Islands of Adventure – CityWalk, a large dining and entertainment district, and three on-site resort hotels.

CityWalk

Lining the waterfront between Universal Studios and Islands of Adventure is CityWalk, a dining and nightlife complex with enough themed bars, restaurants and nightclubs to keep you entertained every night of the week. They include Jimmy Buffett's Margaritaville, the world's largest Hard Rock Café, Pat O'Brien's Orlando (styled after the famous New Orleans original), Bob Marley – A Tribute to Freedom, Nascar Sports Grille, Red Coconut Club and CityJazz.

You can visit CityWalk separately from the parks; there is no admission fee apart from cover charges at some music clubs. It is open from 11am till 2am, and parking is free after 6pm.

SeaWorld

SeaWorld is located in central Orlando, along I-Drive south of the Convention Center. Across the street its smaller sister park, Discovery Cove, offers a more intimate encounter with marine animals; here you can swim with the dolphins, and even spend the day with a trainer. The Aquatica water park opened next door in 2008. All three are owned by Anheuser-Busch, who also operate the Busch Gardens Africa theme park in Tampa.

The Big Splash

When the temperature rises, cool off in the resorts' themed water parks. Disney's Typhoon Lagoon is a topsy-turvy paradise left in the wake of a tropical storm. It features a variety of water slides, a huge surf pool and a chance to snorkel with the sharks at Shark Reef. Only Disney could imagine Blizzard Beach, a summer ski resort created by a freak Florida snowstorm. Among its watery thrill rides is the Summit Plummet, a 120-ft (36-meter) vertical free-falling body slide from top of Mt Gushmore.

Aquatica is SeaWorld's exciting new water park. True to form, the first slide you come to is the Dolphin Plunge, which shoots you right through a pool of Commerson's dolphins. With their black and white markings, they look like miniature killer whales. The park has some killer water slides too, along with a relaxing beach, huge surf pool, a lazy river and colorful kiddie play areas *(see p.68)*.

The world's first water park, Wet 'n Wild, set the bar high when it opened in 1977 with its imaginative thrill slides. Located near Universal Orlando Resort, it continues to devise ever more ingenious ways to spin, twist and scare you silly before plunging you into the water with rides like Bomb Bay *(see p.71)*.

Busch Gardens in Tampa also has an adjoining water park, Adventure Island, open March–October.

Above from far left: time out in Typhoon Lagoon; Summit Plummet is not for the faint-hearted; young Snow White meets her prince.

Day Tripping
Orlando is within half a day's drive of most major destinations in the Sunshine State. With the Atlantic coast just 50 miles (80km) away, you can hit the beach in under an hour. The white sands of the Gulf Coast are 75 miles (120km) away. Other famous places include Miami (230 miles/370km), West Palm Beach (166 miles/270km), Lake Okeechobee (108 miles/174km), and the oldest city in the US, St Augustine (100 miles/160km). The Florida Keys at the southern tip of the state are 370 miles (600km) away.

FOOD AND DRINK

It's not all fast food on the tourist trail. Orlando has a deliciously broad dining scene, from casual, inexpensive eateries to upscale, romantic restaurants with top chefs at the helm. You'll find regional specialties, too – gator tail, anyone?

DOWN HOME AND INTERNATIONAL

With its roots firmly in the South, Orlando has a variety of restaurants serving Southern specialties. There are barbecue joints and casual restaurant-bars where you can sample such down-home delights as alligator, which tastes like a cross between chicken and calamari, and fried catfish. Menus of more upmarket establishments often feature dishes with southern accents, such as pecan-crusted pork or lamb, while the cuisine of the Big Easy is evident in others with such entrées as gumbo, jambalaya and blackened fish or chicken. And for dessert, nearly every restaurant offers their version of that Florida favorite, key lime pie *(see margin, right)*.

Tropical influence

The Caribbean influence is unmist-akeable too, and in many restaurants the decor and menu makes you feel as if you're dining in the tropics. Coconut shrimp is popular as either a starter or main course. So are fish tacos. Many dishes are accompanied by mango salsa or other tropical touches. And thanks to Florida's long association with Cuba, you can sample Cuban

Above: Downtown Disney and CityWalk have restaurants, bars, and clubs all centrally located with transportation back to resort hotels until late evening, so you need not worry about drink-driving.

cuisine more easily here than in most parts of the country.

Something for everyone

The ever-popular American fare of steaks and burgers is ubiquitous all around Orlando, in establishments that vary greatly in price and quality. And with both the Atlantic and the Gulf coasts a stone's throw away, it's not surprising that fish and seafood are highly prevalent too, though they're not necessarily inexpensive. Though there are few vegetarian restaurants per se, most restaurants have at least one or two vegetarian entrées. There are also usually several choices of fresh salads, which come in big portions, or impressively stocked salad bars.

Around the world

Orlando's outlook on cuisine is ever more international. Tapas (or tapas-style) restaurants are highly popular. There are several Japanese restaurants, a Brazilian steakhouse and a Greek taverna. Others serve Middle Eastern, Turkish, French and Mediterranean fare. The ViMi district located north-east of downtown has a growing enclave of Asian restaurants, with Thai, Vietnamese, Chinese and Korean establishments along Colonial Drive

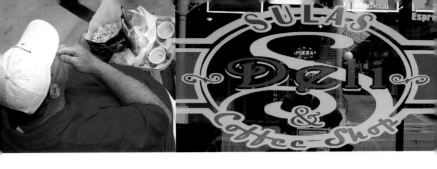

and Mills Avenue. There are a great number of Italian restaurants, ranging from neighborhood pasta and pizza joints to dining rooms with romantic, Old-World decor serving first-class regional dishes.

PLACES TO EAT

Like any large city, Orlando has its hip dining areas. Downtown's Church Street Station is making a comeback with creative restaurants specializing in everything from tapas to dessert. Thornton Park, just east of downtown beyond Lake Eola, has several contemporary restaurants with an urban bistro atmosphere. Winter Park is a long-established favorite for its upscale, quality restaurants, as is Celebration. And many of Orlando's best international establishments can be found along Sand Lake Road's 'Restaurant Row'.

Chain Restaurants

Orlando has a plethora of chain restaurants familiar to every city in the country. Unsurprisingly they are most prevalent along the main tourist drags such as Highway 192 or I-4. All the usual fast-food suspects are here, but others such as Applebee's offer a much wider menu and there's usually something to please every member of the family. Stalwarts like International House of Pancakes (IHOP) or Denny's serve all-day (or all-night) breakfasts. Benigan's is a good bar-restaurant chain with several branches.

Diners

Nostalgic diner-style restaurants are great favorites with both Americans and visitors from overseas. The decor harks back to the 1950s, with jukeboxes, booths, soda fountains and delightful kitsch. Sometimes the waiters and waitresses even get into the act with a song and dance or a beehive hairdo. The food is often nostalgic too, with blue-plate specials like meat loaf, and some of the best burgers, milkshakes and onion rings you'll find anywhere.

Buffet Restaurants

If you're looking for a bargain, look no further than one of Orlando's many buffet restaurants. They range from Chinese buffets to all-you-can-eat seafood and salad bars, pasta bars, Indian lunch buffets, and even lobster feasts.

Above from far left:
cocktail glasses at the ready; ice cream is an after-dinner favorite; fast food is everywhere; Ybor City deli.

Key Lime Pie
The Spanish brought the first key lime trees to the Florida Keys from Malaysia in the 1500s. The fruit is smaller than a golf ball with a yellow-green skin. The first key lime pie was probably made in the late 1800s. Its essential ingredient, apart from key limes, is canned sweetened condensed milk, as the Keys had no fresh milk or refrigeration until the Overseas Highway was built in 1930.

Supermarkets

If you're staying in self-catering accommodation, look for branches of the Publix supermarket chain – there are several in the area. They have a bigger and better selection of foods, including a good deli, and the prices are cheaper than other chains. To find one near you, go to www.publix.com.

Below: waiting for lunch in a pirate-themed restaurant.

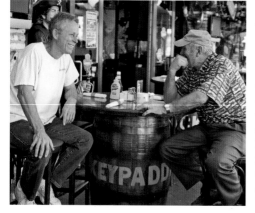

Steakhouses

There are probably more steakhouses in the city than any other type of restaurant (barring fast food), making Orlando a carnivore's delight. Here, as with seafood, you get what you pay for. There are several inexpensive steakhouse chains with big salad bars that cater for families on a budget. If you're a real steak-lover, give them a miss and go for the higher-end, quality restaurants, of which there are several. They offer hand-cut, aged prime beef, oak-grilled, flame-broiled or otherwise cooked to perfection. Most steakhouses also serve a selection of fine seafood.

High-End Restaurants

With more than 50 upscale restaurants within a 10-mile (16-km) radius of the Orange County Convention Center, there are plenty of choices for a memorable meal in Orlando. Several are overseen by internationally acclaimed or celebrity chefs. Menus range from wood-grilled meats to expertly prepared fresh seafood to nouvelle American cuisine with Pacific Rim influences and international accents.

Theme Park and Resort Dining

Though the choice of food is wide, the quality varies enormously at Orlando's theme parks. At the lower end of the scale, the food is often overpriced for what can turn out to be mediocre, mass-produced fare. Go up a notch or two, however, and you can enjoy some excellent meals. It's tough if you only have a day at a park and want to make the most of the attractions, rather than spending time on a sit-down meal. The exceptions are at Epcot's World Showcase and Sea-World, where the quick, lower-priced options are delicious.

Where the parks really excel is in the themed dining and decor. You can dine beside a coral reef, a shark tank or in an African setting. In the Disney parks and some others as well, you can dine with popular characters for breakfast, lunch or dinner at certain restaurants. This is a big hit with families, but should be booked well in advance to avoid disappointment.

Several resort restaurants at the upper end rate among the top fine dining spots in Orlando. Some are in the parks themselves, others are in resort hotels such as the Grand Floridian. The best range of themed restaurants at all price levels can be found in two dining and entertainment enclaves: Downtown Disney and Universal's CityWalk (see p.50).

DRINKS

Alcoholic Drinks

Orlando has all sorts of interesting places to raise a glass of your favorite tipple, from classy lounges to kick-up-your-heels country and western saloons. There are piano bars with dueling pianos and sing-alongs, trendy cigar bars, sports bars and nightclubs offering blues, jazz and rock n' roll. A number of bars have Happy Hour specials on cocktails and bottled beers.

Restaurants and bars often have extensive wine lists with European as well as New World wines. For wine lovers, The Grape at Pointe Orlando and the Eola Wine Company downtown and in Winter Park are two notable wine bars where you can sample a range of fine wines by the glass.

The popularity of micro-breweries has greatly increased the choice of quality beers. English-style pubs serving UK brews are popular, probably no surprise given the high number of visitors from across the pond.

Always take photo identification that gives your birthdate if you want to enjoy an alcoholic drink. You must be 21 years old to drink, and be able to prove it. Even gray-haired pensioners can be 'carded' at any time, and no identification means no booze.

Coffee and Tea

Orlando is a coffee-savvy city, and visitors need no longer suffer the bland, weak drip-filter brews so prevalent across the country. Here, even hotel breakfast buffets often offer quality brands in different strengths to suit everyone's tastes. For coffee shops, the ubiquitous Starbucks is usually never far away. A good alternative is Barnie's, a Florida chain serving very tasty coffee.

You can get hot tea at most cafés and restaurants, and green tea and herbal teas are widely available. Iced tea is an American favorite and, like filter coffee, often comes with free refills. It's often served already sweetened, so if you don't want the sugar specify unsweetened when ordering.

Above from far left: Florida is a paradise for seafood lovers; Glo Lounge on International Drive serves a wide selection of drinks.

Dinner Shows

Dinner shows are a big attraction in Orlando. There are around a dozen of them offering family entertainment from pirate adventures to medieval jousts to luaus, mysteries and magic acts. Most of the dinner shows are fairly pricey, and but don't expect too much from the food. Menus vary according to the theme, but it's hard to mass produce good steaks or chicken and serve it properly in these big theaters. Anyway, the point is not the food but the entertainment, which is also a matter of taste. Many tend towards the corny type of humor. Arabian Nights with its stunning equestrian displays is a long-time favorite. A better bet food-wise is to look for restaurants that also offer entertainment, such as the Columbia Restaurant (see p.121) in Celebration, which has flamenco shows alongside its traditional Cuban cuisine.

SHOPPING

The phrase may be trite, but Orlando really is a shopper's paradise. You'll find everything from mega-malls with the latest fashions and merchandise to designer outlet centers with top name brands at cut-rate prices. Bring an empty suitcase – or just buy one here.

Opening Times
Normal business hours are 9 or 10am until 5 or 6pm. Malls, outlet centers, souvenir shops and many specialty stores stay open much longer, generally opening at 10am and closing between 8 and 10pm Monday–Saturday, with an earlier closing on Sunday.

Orlando has its share of national and international chains. But you can still find one-of-a-kind shops and boutiques scattered around town. Winter Park has the greatest concentration of them along Park Avenue. Celebration has a handful of shops worth browsing, while Downtown Orlando is the place for art galleries and, surprisingly, antiques – along the stretch of Orange Avenue known as Antique Road. Most of America's leading department stores have branches in Orlando's shopping malls.

MALLS AND SHOPPING CENTERS

The Florida Mall (8001 S. Orange Blossom Trail, east of I-Drive) is Orlando's biggest mall, with 260 specialty shops and seven department stores including Nordstrom's, Sak's Fifth Avenue and Dillards. Orlando's latest luxury mall is the Mall at Millenia (4200 Conroy Road), anchored by Neiman Marcus, Macy's and Bloomingdale's with upscale jewelers and designer names among its 150 other stores.

Festival Bay Mall (5250 International Drive) has over 60 stores set around an open-air courtyard. Sprawling outside are several huge specialty stores, including Sheplers Western Wear, Bass Pro Shops Outdoor World, Ron Jon Surf Shop and Surf Park, and Vans Skatepark.

Pointe Orlando (9101 International Drive near the Convention Center) has a mix of shops, boutiques and restaurants including cool clothing stores such as Tommy Bahama and Chico's F.A.S.

OUTLET STORES

Cameras, clothing, luggage, sporting goods, even perfumes – you name it, there's a discount outlet for it somewhere in Orlando. They line the main tourist drags of Highway 192 and I-Drive. Two to look out for are World of Denim, with all the top brand-name jeans at cut prices, and Sports Dominator, with a huge range of quality sportswear and equipment.

There are three big discount outlet open-air malls featuring hundreds of stores with name-brand merchandise. Lake Buena Vista Factory Stores (15657 Apopka Vineland Road) has Eddie Bauer, Tommy Hilfiger, GAP and Van Heusen among its outlets.

Orlando Premium Outlets (8200 Vineland Avenue) has Armani, Calvin Klein, Ann Taylor and Ralph Lauren among its designer names. Prime Outlets International (5401 West Oakridge Road) is the region's largest outlet center, with two malls, annexes and the Designer Outlet Center.

These outlets offer discounts of 25–75 percent, but be aware that the merchandise often differs from the fashions at the regular stores. When buying at the outlet centers, particularly electronic equipment, it pays to know your merchandise and prices, and to avoid being talked into buying alternative items.

FLEA MARKETS AND BARGAIN STORES

For the cheapest deals, visit the International Drive Flea Market (5545 International Drive) or the Osceola Flea Market (2801 East Highway 192, Fri-Sun). Both have hundreds of booths selling all kinds of merchandise. Other bargain stores – often with huge kitschy storefronts – along these roads are good places to pick up cheap beach towels, T-shirts, swimwear, theme park and Florida souvenirs.

SOUVENIRS

It's hard to walk away from the theme parks without a souvenir or cuddly toy in hand. There are some wonderfully creative shops in every park. Downtown Disney's Marketplace is another good hunting ground for unique gifts,

with Once Upon a Toy and World of Disney, its largest shop, among others. The Universal Studios Store at CityWalk has similar themed merchandise. Or check out the Disney Character Outlet at Lake Buena Vista Factory Stores.

FARMERS' MARKETS

There are several farmers' markets and produce markets around Greater Orlando. Winter Park's Farmers' Market is one of the best in central Florida. It is held in the old train depot on New England Avenue opposite Central Park on Saturdays 7am–1pm. Another local favorite takes place at Lake Eola Park in Downtown Orlando, Sunday 10am–4pm. In addition to fresh produce there are gourmet foods from all around the world and interesting arts and craft stalls. Local artists hold an Art Farm here every third Sunday of the month.

Celebration also has a colorful Sunday fruit and vegetable market in the town center from 9am–3pm, and there are arts and crafts activities for kids. The Farmers' Market of Downtown Kissimmee is a more functional mid-week market selling local produce; it operates Thursday 7am–1pm in Toho Square, at the corner of Darlington and Pleasant Street, in the historic downtown area. The landmark giant orange that houses Orange World on Highway 192 is a good place to buy delicious fresh Indian River citrus fruits.

Above from far left: to the gift shop; Orlando fashion; head to Orange World for fresh citrus fruit; crazy display.

What to Buy
Orlando and the coast are perfect places to buy beach gear. Ron Jon Surf Shop is trendy, fun and huge. Cocoa Beach Surf Company in Cocoa Beach has great clothes at lower prices, and an entire shop dedicated to sandals. Cigars are another good buy here, thanks to Florida's Caribbean connections. The Corona Cigar Company has a superstore on Sand Lake Road, or browse the shops in Ybor City, Tampa.

HISTORY: KEY DATES

Long before Europeans appeared on the scene, central Florida was the domain of the Timucua Indians. The Spanish, French and British battled it out for centuries, but it is now Walt Disney who reigns supreme.

EARLY HISTORY

15,000–7,500 BC	Ice-Age glaciers drive Paleo-Indian hunters southwards to the Florida peninsula.
7,500–5,000 BC	North America's first human burials, evidence of which is later found near Cape Canaveral.

COLONIAL TIMES

Above: Seminole man about 1900; Billy Bowlegs, Seminole leader during the Third Seminole War.

1498	John and Sebastian Cabot make first European sighting of Florida at Miami's Key Biscayne.
1513	Juan Ponce de León lands at Cape Canaveral in search of gold and the Fountain of Youth, claiming the territory for Spain.
1562	French settlers build a fort on the St Johns River but are driven out by the Spanish, who found St Augustine.
mid-1700s	Creek Indians – dubbed Seminoles – and runaway African slaves are driven south by American settlers into Florida.
1764–83	Britain rules Florida.
1783	Florida is returned to Spain.
1818	First Seminole War; US General Andrew Jackson campaigns against the Indians in order to take control of Florida.
1819	Spain cedes Florida to the US.
1821–42	Second Seminole War; Seminole leader Osceola is imprisoned and dies a martyr in 1838. Seminoles are driven into the Everglades or are relocated to reservations in Arkansas.

DEVELOPMENT OF ORLANDO

1843	Aaron and Isaac Jernigan found Jernigan settlement, near Fort Gatlin.
1845	Florida becomes a state with 57,921 residents. Mosquito County changes its name to Orange County in an effort to lure settlers.
1857	Jernigan is renamed Orlando.
1870	'Orange fever' takes over and settlers began planting citrus groves in former cotton fields.

1875	Orlando is incorporated (pop. 85), becoming the seat of Orange County.
1880	Henry Plant's South Florida Railroad is extended to central Florida, allowing expansion of Orlando's agricultural markets. The citrus and cattle industries flourish.
1884	Fire destroys most of Orlando's downtown business district.
1887	The first African-American township in the US, Eatonville, is built north of Orlando.
1891	African-American writer Zora Neale Hurston is born in Eatonville.
1894–99	Severe frosts kill 95 percent of Orange County's citrus groves.
1898–9	Florida's links with Cuba via the Tampa cigar factories leads to US troops fighting in Spanish-American War; Cuba wins independence from Spain.

Above from far left:
Walt Disney, brother
Roy, and Governor
Haydon Burns
announce plans for
a new theme park in
Florida; trick photos
were always a popular
tourist souvenir.

20TH CENTURY

1903	First automobile is sold in Orlando; the speed limit is 5mph (8 kph).
1910–25	Land boom hits Florida. 'Tin can tourists' motor to Florida for winter.
1929	Mediterranean fruit flies devastate the citrus industry.
1936	Cypress Gardens opens south of Orlando.
1949	Gatorland opens.
1950s	Post-war automobile tourism skyrockets.
1957	The Glenn L. Martin Company of Baltimore relocates to Orlando, starting a population boom.
1959	Busch Gardens opens in Tampa Bay.
1964–5	Walt Disney secretly buys 47 square miles of rural land and announces plans to build Walt Disney World in Orlando.
1966	Walt Disney dies.
1971	The Magic Kingdom opens.
1973	SeaWorld Orlando opens.
1982	Epcot opens.
1989	Disney Hollywood Studios opens.
1990	Universal Studios opens in Florida.
1998	Animal Kingdom opens.
1999	Islands of Adventure opens.

21ST CENTURY

2000	Discovery Cove opens.
2008	Orlando ranks as the number one Family Spring Break destination in the US.
2009	The Wizarding World of Harry Potter opens at Islands of Adventure.

Crackers
No one knows for
sure why Florida's rural
pioneers were called
'Crackers'. It was
possibly because of
the loud crack of the
wooden whip used
to round up cattle.

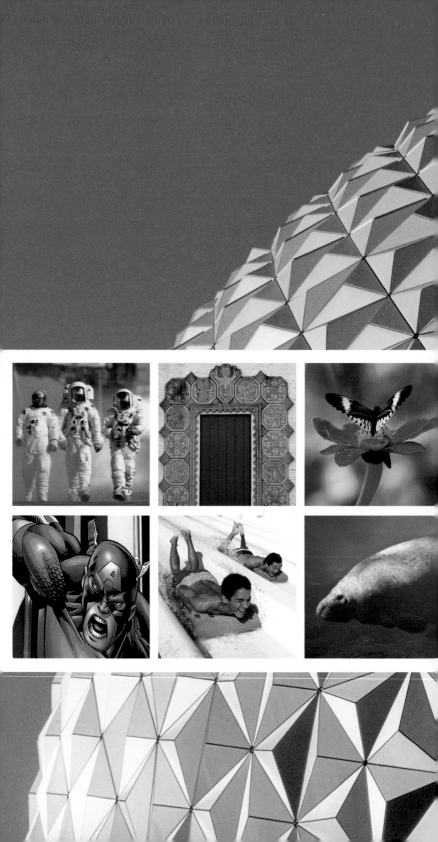

WALKS AND TOURS

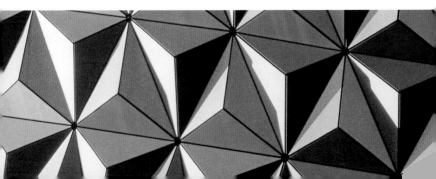

THE MAGIC KINGDOM

This is the theme park that put Orlando on the map, and the one that most visitors head for first. All the classic Disney rides and characters are here, spread throughout the seven lands of the Magic Kingdom which encircle the towering spires of Cinderella's Castle.

PARK SIZE 142 acres
(57 hectares)
TIME One to two days
START/END Main Street USA
POINTS TO NOTE
Arrive early, especially if you only have one day here. Be at the gates at opening time and you'll be able to walk right on to many rides with little or no wait in the first hour or two of the day.

Walt Disney World Resort

Walt Disney World Resort is actually located outside the Orlando city limits, in the cities of Lake Buena Vista and Bay Lake. Covering more than 25,000 acres (100 sq km), it is made up of four theme parks (the Magic Kingdom, Epcot, Animal Kingdom and Disney Hollywood Studios), two water parks (Typhoon Lagoon and Blizzard Beach), the Downtown Disney dining and shopping district, the Pleasure Island nightlife district, DisneyQuest indoor interactive theme park, Disney's Wide World of Sports complex, other sports facilities from golf courses to stock car racing, 33 resort hotels, two spas and even a campground. It really is a world in itself!

As far back as 1959, Walt Disney began scouting for a location to build another theme park, one that would augment Disneyland in California and be more accessible to visitors in the eastern half of the country. In Orlando he found what he was looking for: warm weather, an inland location protected from hurricanes, the intersection of two major highways and an airport.

Disney began buying up land in secret, fearing that prices would skyrocket if word leaked out about his plans. He eventually acquired 47 sq miles (122 sq km) for his 'Florida Project', but it took years to transform the swamp and scrubland into a resort. Walt didn't live to see the realization of his dream. He died in 1966, five years before the Magic Kingdom, Disney's first Florida park, opened.

There's no one best way to tour the Magic Kingdom. The route you take will depend on whether you have children (and their ages), love thrill rides, are a first-time visitor or have more than one day to spend. The best advice for everyone is to arrive early and head for the attraction you most want to see first.

There is only one entrance, which leads into Main Street USA. From here, our tour proceeds clockwise through the other six 'lands', or themed

areas of the park. However, if you have young children you may want to start in Fantasyland, or if you have teenagers, you'll probably head straight to the roller coasters in Frontierland or Tomorrowland. Fastpass times *(see box, p.29)* will also determine how you organize your day.

This tour takes in the highlights of each area, but there are many more shows and attractions besides. Some have different operating hours from the park, so pick up a Times Guide along with a park map at the entrance (or elsewhere around the park), and check the Tip Boards for show times. You won't be able to see everything in one day, so use this tour to help you prioritize the main attractions.

Above from far left: the enduring appeal of Cinderella and Snow White; Main Street USA.

MAIN STREET USA

The stroll down Main Street USA is great for setting the tone of the Magic Kingdom. The neat-as-a-pin storefronts

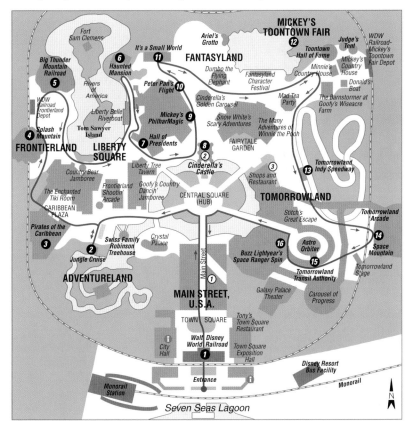

Dreaming Big
'Here in Florida, we have something special we never enjoyed at Disneyland... the blessing of size. There's enough land here to hold all the ideas and plans we can possibly imagine.'
Walt Disney, 1965.

Night Magic
The Magic Kingdom lights up after dark. In peak season, *Spectro-Magic* is an impressive electric parade of Disney characters in glimmering costumes, coaches and floats lit up with fairy lights, fibre optics and holographic images. Line up along Main Street 30–60 minutes in advance for the best viewing spots. *Wishes*, a dazzling fireworks spectacular, explodes most nights over Cinderella's Castle.

and horse-drawn trolleys evoke a small Midwestern town of a century ago, and if it's a bit nostalgic it does the trick of taking you out of your stressed, modern mindset to a simpler place where Disney's imaginary world takes over.

Walt Disney World Railroad
You may want to hop aboard the **Walt Disney World Railroad ❶** for a 20-minute ride around the park. It's a good way of seeing the various lands, or a taking a quick route through the crowd to its other stops at Frontierland and Mickey's Toontown Fair. Otherwise, Main Street USA is mostly lined with shops and eateries – unless you want to have breakfast at the **Main Street Bakery**, see 🍴①, save them for later in the day and continue straight ahead towards Cinderella's Castle.

ADVENTURELAND

Like spokes on a wheel, paths lead out from the hub in front of the castle to the themed lands. Turn left and cross over the bridge to Adventureland, with its atmospheric, semi-tropical setting.

Jungle Cruise
On your left, past the massive Swiss Family Robinson Treehouse, is the entrance to the **Jungle Cruise ❷**. This silly safari takes you down a tropical river past a delightful array of animatronic animals, from giraffes, lions and zebras on the banks to a roaring hippo and a family of elephants bathing in the water. You'll also escape a headhunter or two and sail through a hidden temple. Des-

pite the corny commentary from the captain, it's an amusing ride, so jump on board early when the lines are still short.

Pirates of the Caribbean
From the number of youngsters sporting red-striped bandanas and pirate hats with dangling dreadlocks, it's not hard to guess that one of the most popular attractions is right next door. You'll board another boat for **Pirates of the Caribbean ❸**, this time for a swashbuckling sail through the booming cannons of a pirate raid on a small island town.

This ride into the rollicking world of a pirates' den is a Disney classic, each scene loaded with imaginative detail – watch for the drunken pigs joining in the celebrations. You'll also spot a familiar face among the remarkably lifelike pirates: Johnny Depp's Captain Jack Sparrow. This attraction was in fact the inspiration for the blockbuster *Pirates of the Caribbean* movies.

FRONTIERLAND

Walk through the covered passage into Frontierland, which re-creates rustic settings from America's 19th-century frontier. Two of the park's best thrill rides are located here.

Food and Drink
① MAIN STREET BAKERY
Main Street USA; $
Start the day with a cappuccino and one of the delicious pastries or cakes made here. There are fresh cookies to tempt you back later in the day.

Splash Mountain

Splash Mountain ❹ starts off innocently enough as you ride a log flume past brightly colored scenes from *Song of the South*. Suddenly you emerge at the top of the mountain and plunge down into Brer Rabbit's Laughin' Place with a mighty splash. Those in the front and on the right are sure to get soaked, but it's a great way to cool off on a hot day.

Big Thunder Mountain Railroad

More thrills await at **Big Thunder Mountain Railroad ❺** across the way. The train cars whip round tight curves, through dark tunnels and down into canyons beneath the mountain's red rock spires, said to be modeled after Bryce Canyon in Utah. This ride is exciting but not as terrifying as the big roller coasters, so it's a good option for more timid souls.

LIBERTY SQUARE

The Magic Kingdom's smallest land harks back to colonial times, with an old-fashioned riverboat and 18th-century architecture. Here is one of Disney's best-loved attractions, the **Haunted Mansion ❻**. The ghoulish fun is more clever than scary, full of creepy illusions, gallows humor and animated apparitions, from the diners at a ghostly banquet to the ghost who hitches a ride in your doom buggy.

Hall of Presidents

More in keeping with the theme of Liberty Square is the **Hall of Presidents ❼**. Even if you're not patriotic,

the show is worth seeing for the authentic detail employed to create these animatronic figures, from their period dress to their mannerisms. You can almost believe America's long line of Chief Executives really has assembled on stage for this roll call.

Above from far left:
the Pirates of the Caribbean ship;
a mini Snow White surveys the scene;
high-speed thrills for all the family.

Opening Hours

Opening hours at Disney theme parks vary widely according to the season, the day of the week and special events. They also differ from park to park. Always check on the website or phone ahead when planning your visits: www.disneyworld.com; tel: 407-824-4321. Times for parades, shows and fireworks displays also change frequently. Each park prints a weekly Times Guide for these events. Guests staying at a WDW resort should ask about the Extra Magic Hour program, which gives them early or extended admission before or after park hours. It only applies to certain parks on certain days, and these vary.

Tickets

There are many ticket options for visiting Walt Disney World (WDW) parks, and taking time to think them through is time – and money – well spent. Base tickets are called Magic Your Way and allow entry to one park per day; the cost per day drops the more days you purchase. You can then customize your ticket by adding various options: Park Hopper allows unlimited visits to multiple parks for the length of your ticket, Water Park Fun & More allows a number of visits to other WDW attractions. Unless you buy the No Expiration option, your ticket expires 14 days after first use. Tickets are non-transferable. You can buy tickets at the park entrances, online at www.disneyworld.com, by phone (407-824-4321 or 407-934-7639) or by mail. If you are buying a ticket for four days or more, there is a savings for advance purchase.

Character Greetings
Meeting Mickey
Mouse, Snow White
and other Disney
characters is a big
thrill for most children.
Check the Times
Guide at each park
for Character Greeting
times and places.
But be prepared to
wait in line for a
chance to get Ariel's
autograph or have
your photo snapped
with Donald Duck. You
can also dine with the
characters at several
restaurants in the
parks and resorts, but
you usually need to
book ahead to ensure
a place. For details
and reservations,
tel: 407-WDW-DINE
(407-939-3463).

FANTASYLAND

Continue round the back of **Cin-derella's Castle ❽** to Fantasyland, in many respects the essence of the Magic Kingdom. Although it's the park's landmark, unfortunately the fairytale castle itself isn't open to visitors; you can only enter to dine in the restaurant, **Cinderella's Royal Table**, see ⑪②.

Most of the attractions are based round Disney characters and geared for younger children, but adults are easily charmed by them too. Here you can unashamedly indulge your child-hood fantasies.

Mickey's PhilharMagic

Not to be missed is **Mickey's Philhar-Magic ❾**, arguably the best of the 3D shows in the Disney parks. The 150-foot (50-meter) -wide screen is one of the largest of its kind ever made. Don your 3D glasses and enjoy all kinds of special effects popping literally right before your eyes, as Mickey and com-pany make their own comical brand of musical magic.

Peter Pan's Flight

Next door, **Peter Pan's Flight ❿** is an enchanting ride over London by night to Neverland, with all the characters of this timeless tale. However, it has one of the slowest-moving lines in the park and much of the charm of this popular three-minute ride is lost after lining up for an hour or more. Get there early, or get a Fastpass *(see box, p.29)*.

It's a Small World

Lines move more quickly over the road, as guests board small boats for a leisurely float around the globe in **It's a Small World ⓫**. This audio-animatronic attraction was created for the 1964 World's Fair in New York, though it's since been refurbished. It's still as delightful as ever, with dolls from every country dressed in bright traditional costumes, dancing and singing the catchy theme tune in their own languages. The 10-minute ride is a good chance to cool off and escape from the rush outside.

Wander on past Cinderella's Golden Carrousel – a real one built by Italian carvers in 1917 – and the madly spin-ning teacups of the Mad Tea Party.

MICKEY'S TOONTOWN FAIR

If you have very small children, head into **Mickey's Toontown Fair ⓬**. Here the little ones can explore Mickey and Minnie's Country Houses, cool off in the fountains on Donald's Boat, or ride their first mini roller coaster, the Barn-stormer at Goofy's Wiseacre Farm.

Food and Drink 🍴

② CINDERELLA'S ROYAL TABLE
Cinderella's Castle; tel: 407-939-3463; $$$
Book well ahead to dine at the top venue in the Kingdom, where you'll meet Cinderella and her princesses at breakfast and lunch. The Fairy Godmother makes an appearance at dinnertime.

③ COSMIC RAY'S STARLIGHT CAFÉ
Tomorrowland; $
Probably the widest choice for a fast-food meal, from burgers and hot dogs to barbecue ribs and rotisserie chicken. There are healthy options too, including soups, salads, wraps, and veggie-burgers.

This is also the place where kids can meet Mickey in the Judge's Tent (and parents can snap those priceless photos for the family Christmas card). Other characters are on hand throughout the day in the Toontown Hall of Fame. Be prepared for long waits in line.

TOMORROWLAND

The loud revving of race cars tells you that you've entered the land of the future. Speed freaks may be disappointed that the **Tomorrowland Indy Speedway** ⓭ is not really very fast, but kids love the chance to get behind the wheel.

Space Mountain
Most visitors head straight for **Space Mountain** ⓮, and for many this is a once-in-a-lifetime roller coaster – it's so scary that once in a lifetime is enough. You ride in the dark, through the blackness of outer space with only a few twinkling stars, and as your rocket car soars, dives and whips round tight curves, it feels much faster than its top speed of 28mph (45 kmh). It's the Magic Kingdom's ultimate thrill ride.

Tomorrowland Transit Authority
Celebrate your return to earth at **Cosmic Ray's Starlight Café**, see ⓫③, before taking a calmer ride on the **Tomorrowland Transit Authority** ⓯. This gentle PeopleMover takes you round the land – even into Space Mountain – on an elevated track using a low-power, non-polluting motor. You can usually walk right on.

Buzz Lightyear Space Ranger
For more fun in the dark, ride into outer space on **Buzz Lightyear's Space Ranger Spin** ⓰ to help the *Toy Story* hero save the toy universe from evil Emperor Zurg's robots. Fire your laser cannons, racking up points and setting off sight and sound effects when you hit your celestial targets.

Stroll back down to Main Street USA for a bit of shopping, or find a good spot to take in Disney's night magic *(see margin on p.26)*.

Above from far left: a sprinkling of fairy dust; all on board Aladdin's magic carpet; Prince Charming and his princess; brave souls are amply rewarded.

Beat the Lines

On busy days, waits of 1–2 hours are not uncommon for popular attractions. Use Disney's Fastpass system to make the most of your time. Insert your ticket into the Fastpass machine located near the entrance to many rides, and it will give you a time (usually with an hour's window) when you can return and walk straight onto the ride without waiting in line.

The park maps indicate which attractions have Fastpass options. There is a limited number of Fastpasses each day – they can be gone by noon for some attractions – so head for your favorite ride first. Normally you cannot get a second Fastpass until you've used the first one or the time expires, but for waits of over 2 hours you can sometimes get a second one sooner; if so it will be noted at the bottom of the pass.

EPCOT

More than twice the size of the Magic Kingdom, Epcot is Walt Disney World Resort's biggest theme park. It also has the most appeal for adults, with pavilions dedicated to technology, the land, and world nations that educate as well as entertain.

Epcot Hours
World Showcase opens a couple of hours later than Future World, normally at 11am, and stays open later in the evenings too.

PARK SIZE 305 acres (123 hectares)
TIME One to two days
START/END Spaceship Earth
POINTS TO NOTE
Try to spend two days here if you want to enjoy all the attractions in both sections of the park. The movies and musical entertainment in World Showcase are excellent.

Breakfast Time
Visit The Seas With Nemo & Friends early in the morning when the fish in the Caribbean Coral Reef are usually fed. It's also fun to watch the manatees devouring heads of lettuce for their morning meal.

Walt Disney envisioned a planned residential community that would incorporate the exciting new ideas and technologies that were emerging in the 1960s. He called it the Environmental Prototype Community of Tomorrow. Several years after his death his dream metamorphosed into EPCOT, Disney's second Orlando theme park, which opened in 1982.

There are two very different parts to the park: **Future World** and **World Showcase**. As with the Magic Kingdom, there's no best way to take it all in. It's a long way from one end of the park to the other, so two days here is recommended to see it at a leisurely pace. You don't necessarily need to devote each day to a separate section, but World Showcase in particular is meant for wandering and you don't want to find yourself dashing back for a Fastpass in Future World from the far side of the lagoon.

Since Future World opens earlier than World Showcase it's the logical place to begin. Your interests and the ages of your children will determine your route. Again, head for your must-see attraction first. It's fairly easy to criss-cross this part of the park quickly, and the open spaces, fountains, flowers and brightly colored buildings are delightful. This tour covers the park highlights, beginning with what is arguably its most popular attraction.

FUTURE WORLD

More than 25 years have passed since its opening in 1982, and Epcot's world of the future has become the present. But periodic refurbishments have incorporated new technologies to keep it fresh and up-to-date. Many of the attractions have a timely environmental message which could, frankly, be even stronger and less superficial.

Spaceship Earth
As you enter the park a gleaming sphere resembling a giant golf ball looms before you. This is **Spaceship**

Earth ❶, Epcot's symbol. You may want to save this for later *(see below)*. Inside you board a time machine which transports you through the milestones of communication, with such lifelike scenes as a Greek scholar giving a maths lesson and Michelangelo painting the Sistine Chapel during the Renaissance. You even invent your own future world.

The Land

Even when lines are long at Spaceship Earth, they move fairly quickly for this enjoyable attraction. It's often open late as well. So save it for later and head straight for **The Land ❷**, home of the park's most popular ride.

Soarin', located on the lower floor inside the prism-topped building, is one of Disney's best rides. It simulates a hang-gliding flight across California. Your seat rises 45 feet (14 meters) in the air with nothing but a seat belt between you and the surrounding IMAX screen. With the wind in your face and your feet dangling, you soar upriver over Upper Yosemite Falls, above mountains, redwood forests and Napa Valley vineyards, across the Death Valley desert and in between hot air balloons in flight. It feels so real that as you swoop down over the ocean you automatically lift your feet to avoid hitting the waves.

Fastpasses *(see box, p.29)* go fast here and the day's allotment can be gone by noon. So it's smart to head here first.

In the meantime there's plenty to do nearby. Also in this building is *Living with the Land*, a boat ride through rain forest, desert and prairie landscapes into the greenhouses of a plant research station, where new and innovative varieties of food crops are being cultivated that can help feed the world's growing population and benefit the planet.

The Seas with Nemo & Friends

Turn left out of The Land to visit **The Seas with Nemo & Friends ❸**. Here you can take a fun ride in a clamshell through Nemo's underwater world, with the cartoon characters superimposed into the real aquarium at the end.

Above from far left: Epcot's famous landmark; a monorail connects Epcot with the Magic Kingdom, making a handy way to travel between the parks; hang-gliding over San Francisco's Golden Gate Bridge.

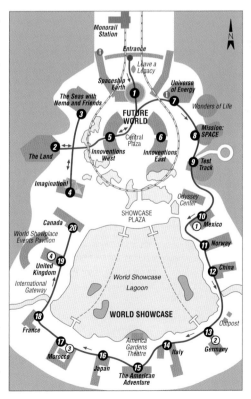

Behind the Scenes Tours
Behind the Seeds: a closer look at the hydroponic gardens and fish farm in The Land. **Epcot Seas Aqua Tour**: snorkel with Nemo and friends in their underwater world.
DiveQuest: a swim with the sharks and other aquarium dwellers, for certified scuba divers.
Dolphins in Depth: learn about dolphin behaviour and watch the trainers at work. For information on these and other tours, tel: 407-WDW-TOUR (407-939-8687).

Below: Venetian carnival at the Italy pavilion.

You can while away hours in this pavilion watching the manatees, dolphins, sharks, and seahorses. The huge Caribbean Coral Reef holds real-life Nemos (clownfish) and over 60 species of sea creatures. There's also an entertaining interactive show, *Turtle Talk With Crush*.

Imagination!

Make your way to the other side of The Land, dodging – or cooling off in – the whimsical Jellyfish and Leap Frog fountains outside the **Imagination!** pavilion ❹. These twin glass pyramids contain the *ImageWorks* labs, with games and activities to stretch the imagination, and a journey with the purple dragon Figment.

The highlight here is the 3D show, *Honey I Shrunk the Audience*, featuring the hapless Professor Wayne Szalinski. As his latest invention goes hilariously (and convincingly) wrong, you'll be assaulted by an army of mice, an escaped snake and a malicious five-year-old while in your miniature state.

Innoventions West

Stroll back across the central plaza, where you can explore a variety of technologies in two pavilions. Among those contained in **Innoventions West ❺** are Segway Central where you can learn to ride the motorized scooters; a computer bank with Disney Pixar animation, Rockin' Robots, and the Think-a-ma-Jig computer game.

Innoventions East

Innoventions East ❻ offers an exhibit on recycled paper, and more dated displays on plastics, manufacturing test labs and the like. These exhibits are sponsored by large corporations, as are others around Epcot, and the unavoidable corporate message can be annoying in what should be a commercial-free zone.

Universe of Energy

Continue round to **Universe of Energy ❼**, which houses *Ellen's Energy Adventure*. The corny storyline takes comedienne Ellen DeGeneres back to prehistoric times, and while the dinosaurs are good, the lack of any mention of energy conservation is disappointingly out of step with today's world, let alone tomorrow's.

Mission: SPACE

Hurry on to one of Epcot's most exciting attractions, **Mission: SPACE ❽**.

Blast off to Mars in a simulator that recreates the feeling of space flight, including the G-force, spinning and sense of weightlessness (and for some people, the motion sickness as well). Astronauts say it's amazingly close to the real experience. For those who don't feel up to chancing the full-on Orange version, there's a less intense Green version that eliminates the spinning and is just as much fun.

Test Track

For more vehicular thrills, **Test Track** ❾ is right next door. This ride through an automobile proving ground is a must for anyone who loves cars and speed. You'll see and feel how acceleration, brakes, suspension, steering and other systems are rigorously tested as you zoom around the track at up to 65 mph (100 kmh).

WORLD SHOWCASE

This section of the park is set around the World Showcase Lagoon, a circular body of water covering nearly 40 acres (16 hectares). It's about 1.2 miles (2 km) around, but the promenade is pleasantly broad and made for strolling. You can also take a *Friend-Ship* water taxi across the lagoon, though this isn't a speedier option.

Each of the 11 pavilions represents a nation of the world, showcasing its landmarks, architecture, arts, food, drink and, of course, its wares. Some of the pavilions also have rides, films and cultural exhibits in addition to shops and restaurants. The Circle-Vision 360

films are particularly impressive. World Showcase also has some of the best food in the entire resort, so this is the place to indulge.

Best of all are the pavilions themselves. Each is an impressively detailed rendition of the landmarks, buildings, squares, and other elements that represent a country's culture and history. You can spend hours here just leisurely browsing and admiring the artful features you see.

Mexico, Norway, and China

This tour proceeds clockwise around the lagoon, beginning with **Mexico** ❿. Inside the striking Aztec pyramid are shops and cultural exhibits set

Above from far left: cocktail time at the Mexico pavilion; Figment the purple dragon; laughing dolphin; on their way to Mission:Space.

IllumiNations

Don't miss Epcot's nighttime extravaganza, IllumiNations – Reflections of Earth. The 15-minute show is a mixture of fireworks, lasers, colors, fountains, and lights, set to music and centered on an enormous globe in the middle of the lagoon. It's visible from all around the promenade – anywhere where you can see both the water and the sky – but stake your spot at least 30 minutes in advance. Good viewing spots include Showcase Plaza (at the bridge with Future World) and the Rose & Crown Pub in the United Kingdom.

World Crew
Many of the cast members (as all Disney employees are called) in the pavilions at World Showcase are natives of the country they represent. Shops sometimes feature visiting artists demonstrating crafts from their homeland.

Below right:
St Mark's Square in Epcot's Venice.

around a Mexican-style plaza. You can take a labyrinthine boat ride with *The Three Caballeros*, which floats through the romantic **San Angel Inn** restaurant, see ⑪①.

A Viking longboat and a beautiful wooden stave church are highlights of the town square in **Norway** ⑪. *Maelstrom* takes you through stormy seas in a dragon-headed boat.

With its circular temple, landscaped gardens and soft, traditional music, **China** ⑫ is an oasis of tranquillity. *Reflections of China*, a stunning CircleVision 360 film, completely surrounds you with images from this truly beautiful ancient land. It's one of the best in the park.

Germany and Italy

The main attraction in **Germany** ⑬ is the **Biergarten restaurant**, see ⑪②. Shops are set around a statue of St George in the half-timbered square.

An amazing re-creation of St Mark's Square in Venice, with exquisite architectural detail in everything from the Doge's Palace to the statues, makes **Italy** ⑭ one of the finest pavilions here. The Italian shops and restaurants are secondary to the scenery.

The American Adventure

Be ready for a big dollop of patriotism at **The American Adventure** ⑮, from the fife and drum corps marching outside the colonial-style pavilion to the

Food and Drink

① SAN ANGEL INN
Mexico Pavilion; $$
Authentic Mexican food served in the shadow of a Mayan temple and a smoldering volcano. The dim lighting makes a good option for couples hoping for a bit of romance.

② BIERGARTEN RESTAURANT
Germany Pavilion; $$
This buffet-style restaurant, set in a dimly lit mock-timber house, serves bratwurst and an array of German fare. The healthy selection of beers will get you in the mood for the live Bavarian music.

③ TANGIERINE CAFÉ
Morocco Pavilion; $
A great place for tabbouleh, cous cous salad, kebabs and other Moroccan dishes, which you can eat at outdoor tables beneath the tiled arches.

④ ROSE & CROWN PUB AND DINING ROOM
United Kingdom; $–$$
Bass ale, Guinness stout and traditional pub grub – fish-andchips, meat pies, ploughman's lunches and even sticky toffee pudding – ensure this popular watering hole is busy throughout the day. Try for a waterside table.

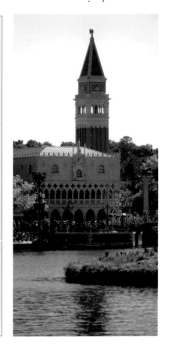

Voices of Liberty, a capella group singing patriotic songs inside. That aside, *The American Adventure* show does an admirable job of covering highlights in American history in 26 minutes, with a cast of superb audio-animatronic characters led by Ben Franklin and Mark Twain.

Japan, Morocco, and France

Japan ⓰ is another tranquil spot, with beautifully landscaped grounds, a pagoda and striking Japanese architecture. The Bijutsu-Kan Gallery houses cultural exhibits.

Beautiful handmade mosaic tiles were used to construct the fine replicas of the Koutoubia Minaret and Bab Boujouloud arched gate in **Morocco** ⓱. Behind is a winding souk where you can get authentic wares from carpets to henna tattoos. Guided tours of the pavilion highlight the country's culture and history. The **Tangierine Café**, see ⑪③, offers quick and tasty Moroccan dishes which you can eat at outdoor tables.

If you've been to Paris you'll enjoy the **France** ⓲ pavilion's pastiche of this great city, from the Eiffel Tower to the Belle Epoque architecture. And of course, it has two of Epcot's best restaurants and a patisserie. *Impressions de France*, one of the park's finest films, takes you on a tour of the French countryside set to stirring music by French composers.

UK and Canada

Cross the replica Pont des Arts to the **United Kingdom** ⓳, where the country's history is represented by a thatched cottage, castle, Georgian square, Tudor chimneys, half-timbered and Victorian buildings. There's even a pair of the traditional red phone boxes that are a rarity in Britain itself these days. Naturally, the main attractions are the **Rose & Crown pub**, see ⑪④, and the fish and chip shop.

An imposing totem pole marks the entrance to **Canada** ⓴, alongside a trading post and Rocky Mountain waterfall with the Hôtel du Canada rising up behind. The Circle-Vision 360 film *O Canada!* is an impressive look at the wildlife, people, cities and extraordinary landscapes of this vast and varied nation.

Above from far left: trying on hats at the Chinese pavilion; large wood carvings.

Epcot Entertainment
Most pavilions have performances all day-long and into the evening, listed in the park's Times Guide. Among the highlights are Off Kilter's rockin' bagpipes (Canada), Beatles hits from the British Invasion (United Kingdom), Japan's Matsuriza drummers, China's Dragon Legend Acrobats and the Mariachi Cobre band (Mexico).

Special Events

Foodies take note! A great time to visit Epcot is during the International Food and Wine Festival, held each year from late September to early November. Even more countries join the culinary array in World Showcase, with top chefs, tastings, wine, and cooking classes. Keen gardeners should time their visit for the International Flower & Garden Festival, mid-March through May, with stunning floral and topiary displays, workshops, and tips from gardening experts.

3

DISNEY HOLLYWOOD STUDIOS

Hollywood helped make Walt Disney famous, and this theme park celebrates the magic of the movies. From the backlot tour to stunt show spectaculars to thrill rides and the resort's biggest nighttime extravaganza, Mickey pulls a whole lot of enchantment out of his sorcerer's hat.

Walt and Oscar
Walt Disney earned more Academy Award Oscars than any other person in motion picture history. He was nominated 63 times for work ranging from animation to documentaries and live action short subjects, and won 26 awards, beginning with an Honorary Oscar for the creation of Mickey Mouse in 1931. In 1941 he received the Irving G. Thalberg Memorial Award, given to a creative producer responsible for consistently high-quality motion picture production – considered to be the industry's highest accolade.

PARK SIZE 135 acres (54 hectares)
TIME One day
START Hollywood Boulevard
END Hollywood Hills Amphitheater
POINTS TO NOTE
Get here at least 30 minutes in advance (more on busy days) to claim a good seat for the stunt shows and *Fantasmic!*

Disney's third Florida theme park made its debut in May 1989 as Disney-MGM Studios, after a neck-and-neck race with Universal Studios to open first (Disney won by a hair). Both companies had been simultaneously developing plans for a movie-themed park for a great number of years, but they have evolved into very different creatures, each with their own unforgettable attractions.

In January 2008, the park changed its name to Disney Hollywood Studios. With neon-lit Art-Deco movie palaces lining Sunset Boulevard, it reflects Tinseltown's heyday of the 1930s and '40s.

Smaller than the other Disney parks, this one can easily be seen in a day. But the park areas are less defined, and you will spend a fair amount of time navigating back and forth to hit the show times. Shows are a big part of Disney Hollywood Studios, and their schedules will largely determine your tour route. It's a good idea to spend a few minutes with a Times Guide when you enter the park to work out which shows you want to see, and plan your day around them.

The park's icon, a giant replica of the sorcerer's hat worn by Mickey in his sorcerer's apprentice role in *Fantasia*, acts as a central hub, with thrill rides to the right and stunt shows and studio tours to the left as you approach

Food and Drink
① **50S PRIME TIME CAFÉ**
Echo Lake; $–$$
At this reincarnation of mom's kitchen, waiters discipline anyone who does not clean their plate, or is caught with elbows on the table. The food is just what you'd expect from mom too: meatloaf, peas, pot roast, fried chicken, and indulgent desserts you choose from a retro Viewmaster toy.

from Hollywood Boulevard. This tour proceeds in a roughly clockwise direction around the park, to end at the Hollywood Hills ampitheater for a fabulous finale.

LIGHTS, CAMERA, ACTION

Walk up **Hollywood Boulevard** ❶ towards the Sorcerer's Hat. The stage in front is used for musical productions – currently *High School Musical 2: School's Out* – several times a day.

Turn left and walk past Echo Lake. Note that on the opposite side of the lake is a great lunch spot to return to later, the **50s Prime Time Café**, see ⑪①. For now, carry on to the **Indiana Jones Epic Stunt Spectacular** ❷. This exciting show re-creates action scenes from the popular Indiana Jones movies, and afterwards demonstrates how the furious fights and great escapes are achieved.

Opposite is **Sounds Dangerous – Starring Drew Carey** ❸, a continually running show which explores the audio effects of filmmaking with special 3-D headsets.

Further on is **Star Tours** ❹, a long-running favorite based on the *Star Wars* movies. After booking a flight with the familiar robots R2-D2 and C-3PO, you board a spacecraft for what becomes a wild intergalactic ride. The flight simulator pitches and tilts as it dodges laser blasts and other hazards, creating a turbulently realistic and thrilling ride.

Come back down to earth with a laugh in a nearby courtyard. Behind

the whimsical Muppets fountain is the continuously running show, **Muppet*Vision 3-D** ❺. This entertaining production with the Muppet characters mixes 3-D film, audio-animatronics and all kinds of special effects. Watch out for the cream pies!

For more movie magic, wander through the **Streets of America** ❻, a corner of the park lined with a variety

Above from far left: Mickey Mouse appeal; *High School Musical* soars to life with a dazzling new show of singing and dancing; meet Lightning McQueen from *Cars*; learn all about the world of action stunts.

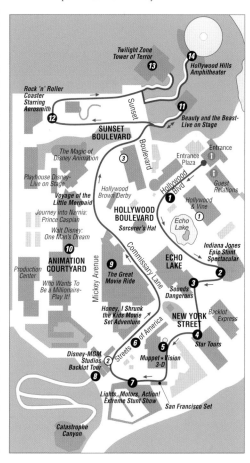

Above from left to right: the streets of San Francisco; Ingrid Bergman and Humphrey Bogart appear in The Great Movie Ride; the Extreme Stunt Show.

of movie backdrops. The San Francisco street scene, which appears to be running uphill towards the Golden Gate Bridge, is most impressive.

More awesome tricks of the movie trade are revealed at the **Lights, Motors, Action! Extreme Stunt Show ❼**. After watching high-speed (and loud) car and motorcycle chases through airborne jumps and flaming explosions, you'll find out how these expert drivers manage to come out unscathed. Seating is limited for this attraction and Fastpasses aren't always available, so get there early.

If you've worked up an appetite, head for **Studio Catering Co.**, see ⓧ②, nearby. Tucked away behind various buildings is the entrance to the **Studio Backlot Tour ❽**, a 35-minute walking and tram tour that takes you behind the scenes to the wardrobe, prop and lighting departments, the scene shop, urban facades and special effects areas. Guides point out the Earful Tower, a replica of the

Getting in on the Action
If you've always wondered what it would be like to be a movie 'extra', you may get your chance at the Indiana Jones stunt show. A few lucky audience members are chosen at random, and after going backstage for costumes and rehearsal, they turn up onstage during the show. Get there early and sit near the front to increase your chances.

water tower on Disney's California backlot. The highlight of the tour is a trip through Catastrophe Canyon, where the tram is caught in a flash flood and flaming oil field explosion.

MOVIE HEAVEN

Walk back through more Streets of America facades and turn left along Commissary Lane. Behind the Sorcerer's Hat is a replica of one of Hollywood's most famous landmarks, Mann's Chinese Theatre, which contains **The Great Movie Ride ❾**.

This attraction is an adult's delight. Many a grinning baby boomer can be seen bouncing along to the Sorcerer's Apprentice theme tune from *Fantasia*, before boarding a car and disappearing beneath a glittering marquee for a nostalgic ride through the classic movies of their youth. There are scenes from *Mary Poppins*, *Casablanca*, *Tarzan*, *Alien*, and others featuring John Wayne, Clint Eastwood, and James Cagney. A highlight is the Munchkinland scene from the *Wizard of Oz*, with a scary appearance by the Wicked Witch of the West.

Continue around the hat and through the archway into the **Animation Courtyard ❿**. Here you can see how Disney's animated characters are drawn, or join Ariel in her underwater world for the delightful show, *Voyage of the Little Mermaid*. For an insight on the man who started it all, browse the exhibits in *Walt Disney: One Man's Dream*.

Take a stroll down Sunset Boulevard; with its Art-Deco movie palaces,

Food and Drink ⓧ

② STUDIO CATERING CO.
Streets of America; $–$$
The full-service bar is a great accompaniment to pulled pork and other specialty sandwiches, grilled chicken with black beans and rice, salads, and desserts.

③ CATALINA EDDIE'S
Sunset Boulevard; $
The best of the lot in this fast-food court at this end of the park. Serves pizzas, Caesar salads, as well as deli sandwiches.

it's one of the most atmospheric streets in the park. Among the cluster of fast-food restaurants, **Catalina Eddie's**, see ⑪③, is a good option. On the right is the Theater of the Stars, where **Beauty and the Beast** ⑪, a live musical show, is performed several times a day. It's well worth seeing this colorful production, and the palace scenes with the singing-dancing teapot, clock and candlestick are especially delightful.

At the end of the street, turn left for the park's biggest thrill ride, the **Rock 'n' Roller Coaster Starring Aerosmith** ⑫. Racing from 0 to 60mph (100kmh) in 2.8 seconds, it is the resort's fastest roller coaster. Your stretch limo car carries on to the party through loops and corkscrew turns, while blasting the band's rock hits at high volume.

Looming over the park at the end of Sunset Boulevard is the Hollywood Tower Hotel, home of the **Twilight Zone Tower of Terror** ⑬. Inside you'll take an elevator ride through eerie scenes reminiscent of the classic TV series. Amid random drops the ride culminates in a 13-story plunge from the top of the tower.

Another path leads to the **Hollywood Hills Amphitheater** ⑭. This is the setting for Disney's best nighttime show, *Fantasmic!*. From atop a mountain in the middle of the lake, Mickey conjures up an extravaganza of lasers, lights, dancing fountains, fireworks, a menacing dragon, king cobra, and a shipful of Disney characters. It's an amazing production of special effects, choreographed to music – don't miss it.

New Attractions

As we went to press, two new attractions were scheduled to open in 2008. *Toy Story Mania* is an interactive ride in which guests wear 3-D glasses and ride through a series of midway-style games, aiming at animated targets and scoring points. Later in the year, a new 'American Idol' attraction will give guests the chance to audition and perform on stage in a competition modeled after the popular TV show.

Left: The *High School Musical* movies are a Disney success story: go Wildcats!

ANIMAL KINGDOM

Real animals are the stars at Disney World's fourth theme park, though a couple of thrill rides and a menagerie of Disney characters have been added to the mix. Go on a safari through the African plains, explore a jungle trail and take in two of the most colorful stage shows in the resort.

Creature Comforts
Animal welfare is paramount at Animal Kingdom. The park generally closes earlier than the other parks in the resort, and even on late nights the animals are brought in at their regular time to avoid stress. This is also the only park without a fireworks show, as it could be distressing to many park residents.

PARK SIZE 403 acres (163 hectares)
TIME One to two days
START Oasis
END Discovery Island
POINTS TO NOTE
You can see all the highlights of the park in one day, especially if you don't have children, but you can spend hours just watching the more fascinating animals; allow two days if you want to take your time.

Animal Kingdom is different from the other Disney theme parks. Opened in 1998, its focus is on animal conservation and letting visitors experience the wonder of the creatures who share our planet. Walt Disney himself was a keen proponent of conservation back in the 1940s and 1950s and won several Academy Awards for his documentaries on the natural world.

At more than 400 acres (1.6 sq km) Animal Kingdom is the largest of Disney's parks anywhere, but most of the land is devoted to naturalistic habitat for the animals. Some 250 species live in seemingly open and impressively landscaped surroundings, giving visitors a sense of exploration as they search for the inhabitants along well-blended trails and paths. Most animals have space to roam (and space to hide), and nowhere does it feel like a zoo.

The hub of the park is Discovery Island. Its centerpiece is the enormous Tree of Life, the park's icon. From here bridges lead across the Discovery River to the other six themed sections of the park.

It's a good idea to head for the Kilimanjaro Safari first: lines are shorter and the animals generally more active in the morning than in the heat of the day. Or, if thrill rides are your thing, make your way to Asia for a Fastpass.

Also pick up the Times Guide along with the park map at the entrance, and check the show times. There are fewer shows here than at the other parks, but *Flights of Wonder*,

---

Food and Drink 🍴
① RAINFOREST CAFÉ
Oasis; tel: 939-9100; www.rainforest cafe.com; $$
You may be familiar with this chain's animatronic animals and faux decor that re-creates a rainforest canopy. Instead of an iguana burger and plantains, expect typical American food in large portions. Waits of an hour or more are not uncommon without reservations.

Finding Nemo – The Musical and *Festival of the Lion King* are all unmissable attractions. It's worth planning your day to fit them all in.

This tour proceeds clockwise around the park through the seven lands, noting the top attractions. Near the entrance is the **Rainforest Café**, see ⓘ, which you can enter from inside and outside the park.

OASIS

Shortly after the entrance gates you enter this small and gentle land. Just like on a real safari, guests often rush through here in pursuit of bigger game. But the **Oasis Exhibits** ❶ repay those who linger with a collection of fascinating animals including warthogs, giant anteater, wallabies, and Hyacinth macaw. The calming landscape of lush foliage, pools, and waterfalls helps you change gear, ready for the natural world that lies ahead.

DISCOVERY ISLAND

Cross the bridge to Discovery Island. It may not be nature's handiwork, but the 14-story **Tree of Life** ❷ is a wonder to behold. Disney artists took more than a year to create this artificial banyan tree, carving some 325 birds, bugs, mammals and reptiles into its 8,000 branches. See how many you can spot along the Discovery Island trails which wind around its base.

Also here is the entertaining 3-D movie, **It's Tough to be a Bug!** ❸. Most adults and older kids love it, but

the sounds, smells, and other special effects can be quite startling and may upset young children or those with a strong aversion to creepy-crawlies.

CAMP MINNIE-MICKEY

If you have young children, cross the bridge into this land where several Greetings Trails lead to meetings with Mickey, Minnie, and other favorite Disney characters. There is also the children's show *Pocahontas and Her Forest Friends*.

Above from far left: giraffe on the Kilimanjaro Safari; jungle fever; the golden lion tamarin, a small monkey now very rare in the wild; zebras are much more common.

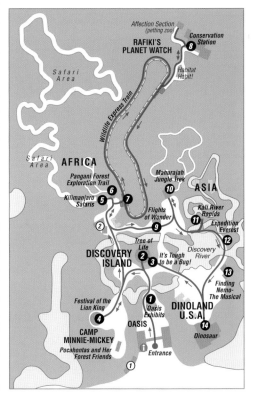

Above from left to right: the Festival of the Lion King; braving it down the Kali River Rapids.

Disney's Big Splash
When the temperature rises, cool off in one of the resort's two themed water parks. Typhoon Lagoon is a topsy-turvy paradise left in the wake of a tropical storm. It features a variety of water slides, a huge surf pool and a chance to snorkel with the sharks at Shark Reef. Only Disney could imagine Blizzard Beach, a summer ski resort created by a freak Florida snow-storm. Among its watery thrill rides is the Summit Plummet, a 120-ft (36-meter) vertical free-falling body slide from the top of Mt. Gushmore.

Adults, however, need only enter the camp to see the **Festival of the Lion King ❹**, an energetic and colorful live show based on the hit musical. The bright flamboyant tribal costumes, giant mechanical animals, gymnastics, singing and dancing make for an outstanding production.

AFRICA

Cross back to Discovery Island and continue on into Africa. Here the Animal Kingdom comes into its own. At **Kilimanjaro Safaris ❺** you take a realistically bumpy ride in an open-air safari vehicle out into landscape reminiscent of an African savannah. The animals roam freely, but you're fairly certain to see elephants, giraffe, zebra, and various breeds of antelope. Lions, black rhino, white rhino and hippos may be more elusive.

What is a fascinating journey in itself is unfortunately 'Disney-fied' by a silly (and jolting) chase after so-called ivory poachers. More commentary on the animals you've come to see would be more rewarding. As animals – and thus safaris – are always unpredictable, you will see different things at different times of day, so consider riding twice if time allows. Generally, more animals

will be active in early morning and late evening than in the midday heat.

After all that bouncing around you'll be glad to put your feet on solid ground and wander the **Pangani Forest Exploration Trail ❻** at your own pace. Gorillas are the highlight here, though when it's hot they may spend much of the day curled up in the shade in the dense vegetation. Another treat is the underwater hippo viewing area, where it's fascinating to see these great beasts taking a swim.

The **Tusker House**, see ⓪②, opposite houses a buffet restaurant.

RAFIKI'S PLANET WATCH

Board the **Wildlife Express Train ❼** for the short ride to this separate area of the park, with a peek at some of the behind-the-scenes animal enclosures on the way. The main attraction here is the **Conservation Station ❽**, with interactive exhibits on wildlife and habitats, veterinary care and research, designed to encourage conservation awareness. There is also a petting zoo for children and displays on how to attract animals to your own backyard habitat.

Return by train to the station, then make your way to the river's shore and turn left.

ASIA

As Africa gives way to Asia, duck into the open-air theater for **Flights of Wonder ❾**, an amazing show where a variety of birds demonstrate their intelligence and aerial prowess. Feath-

---

Food and Drink 🍴
② TUSKER HOUSE
Africa; $$
A good all-you-can-eat buffet of carved meats, salads, and desserts is served inside at lovely carved tables or outdoors under a thatched roof. There's also a character breakfast, but book ahead for that one.

ered performers range from a grape-snatching hornbill to a swooping crowned crane to hawks, eagles, owls, and macaws. The chance to see these great birds up close and uncaged is wonderful indeed.

Discover Komodo dragons and other exotic Asian creatures on the **Maharajah Jungle Trek ⑩**. Wander at your own pace through a Southeast Asia rain forest setting. Bengal tigers lounge against the walls of an ancient ruined palace or come right up to inspect you through the glass as if *you* were the specimen *they've* come to see. There's no barrier, however, between you and the giant fruit bats hanging round the corner, lazily stretching their 6-foot (2-meter) wingspans.

Asia is also the site of two thrill rides. **Kali River Rapids ⑪** is a sure way to cool off as you ride the white-water raft through an endangered rain forest, literally soaking up the adventure. Looming above the eastern side of the park is the snow-capped peak of **Expedition Everest – Legend of the Forbidden Mountain ⑫**. Board the train for a high-speed roller-coaster ride down the rugged slopes into the land of the Yeti.

DINOLAND USA

A prehistoric theme takes over across the bridge in Dinoland USA. The Theater in the Wild is home to the fabulous stage show **Finding Nemo – The Musical ⑬**. Live actors wielding character puppets (the jellyfish are positively enchanting) and a charming story set to an original musical score make this an unforgettable production.

Much of this land has a carnival park feel, with kiddie rides and midway games. Younger children enjoy digging in the Boneyard. The biggest thrill here for anyone over 10 is **Dinosaur ⑭**, a scary dark ride that takes you back in time to rescue DNA from the last iguanodon. You'll encounter some moving, breathing, fiercely realistic dinosaurs on this jarring prehistoric time trip.

Stroll back across the bridge to Discovery Island, and end your visit in more tranquil surroundings beneath the Tree of Life.

DisneyQuest

Just because you've visited all four theme parks, you haven't quite 'done Disney World'. There's one more indoor theme park: DisneyQuest. Located in Downtown Disney, it features five floors of high-tech, interactive games and rides. Among the highlights is Pirates of the Caribbean, where you take to the high seas to bag some booty, firing cannon-balls and fending off attackers in an amazing pirate ship simulator. Or try the space-age bumper cars in Buzz Light-year's AstroBlaster. You can even design your own roller coaster on CyberSpace Mountain. Disney Quest (daily 11.30am–11pm, Fri–Sat until midnight; charge) can be visited separately or as part of a resort package.

Left: Finding Nemo – The Musical.

WELCOME TO THE SET!

UNIVERSAL MONSTE

5 UNIVERSAL STUDIOS

Amid the thrill rides, cartoon characters, shows and attractions, you may come across the next hit movie being made, for Universal Studios is a working film studio as well as a theme park.

TIME One day
START Production Central
END Hollywood
POINTS TO NOTE
With careful planning, in a long day you can hit most of the highlights here and also take in some of the rides at Islands of Adventure. But if you want to take in all the shows, it's best to allow two days here.

Special Events
From February through mid-April is Mardi Gras at Universal Studios, with parades and live music concerts on Saturday nights. Entrance is included with admission to the park. Similar Halloween Horror events are held in October.

Universal Studios is a theme park for everyone who loves movies. While the rides and attractions feature plenty of popular film characters, it is not as character-led as the Disney parks and has a very different, earthier feel. Facades here look like authentic back-lots and behind-the-scenes action attractions like Twister really let you experience how movies are made. The fact that the film studios here opened in 1988, two years before the theme park, gives it added authenticity.

That said, when it comes to fun and entertainment, Universal Studios puts on a star performance. Twice the size of its California counterpart, it is one of the world's most popular parks. Its adjoining sister park, Islands of Adventure, has some seriously scary thrill rides. Together with the 30-acre (12-hectare) CityWalk dining and nightlife complex *(see p.50)* in between, they make up Universal Orlando resort.

It's easy to get around the park, so your interests and the show times will largely determine your route. The three most popular rides are Men in Black, Revenge of the Mummy and Shrek. On busy days, head for these first. This tour describes the highlights of the many shows and attractions, proceeding in a clockwise direction from the entrance.

PRODUCTION CENTRAL

From the entrance gate walk up Plaza of the Stars. On your left is **Jimmy Neutron's Nicktoon Blast ❶**, based on Nickelodeon's cartoon hero (programming for this cable network was produced here for 15 years). This ride uses a superb flight simulator and animated graphics to make you feel you're

Right: meet Bullwinkle.

zooming through space with the boy genius in pursuit of a stolen rocket ship.

Over the road is **Shrek 4-D ❷**, a delightful movie in which special effects let you join the gentle ogre and Princess Fiona on their ill-fated honeymoon.

NEW YORK

Walk up 57th Street into New York, a backlot with some marvelous facades of the Big Apple. On your left, see – and

feel – just how natural disaster movie scenes are created in **Twister... Ride It Out ❸**. As the wind roars, gas tanks burst into flame and a cow flies by in the whirlwind, the sensation of being caught in a tornado is all too real. Your feet may never leave the ground but the special effects will blow you away.

At the end of the street, The Vinyls play classic rock 'n' roll on the steps of the New York Public Library in the **50's Street Bash ❹** – grab a hoola hoop and

Above from far left: welcoming youngsters to a playground; at the Monsters' Café you can eat surrounded by memorabilia from classic horror flicks; the vintage streets of New York.

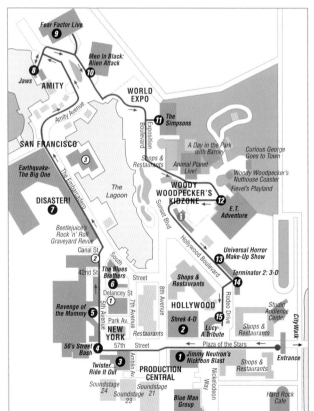

Express Plus
Universal Studios and Islands of Adventure have an Express Plus system that lets you use the Express entrance and bypass the lines at most rides and attractions. It's free if you're staying at a Universal Orlando resort, but all visitors can purchase the pass for an additional fee. Single riders can also move through the lines more quickly by taking up spare seats in roller coaster cars and other rides. Ask the ride attendant.

Blue Man Group
Universal Orlando is the perfect home for the Blue Man Group *(pictured below)*, who now perform their phenomenal stage show in a dedicated theater adjacent to the Universal Studios entrance. Their blend of music, humor and theatrical percussion instruments makes for a truly unique and unforgettable show.

join in. Around the corner more thrills await in the park's biggest ride, **Revenge of the Mummy ⑤**, where you'll plunge into a tomb of darkness on a roller coaster through balls of fire and fearsome warriors from the dead.

Nearby on Delancey Street, Jake and Elwood strut their stuff across from **Finnegan's Bar and Grill**, see ⑪①, in a rockin' rendition of **The Blues Brothers ⑥** famous hits. Continue along 5th Avenue to **Louie's Italian Restaurant**, see ⑪②, where you can stop for lunch, perhaps over more music if Beetlejuice's Graveyard Revue is performing across the street.

SAN FRANCISCO/AMITY

Walk on into San Francisco along the Embarcadero. Notice the turntable in the middle of the cobbled street, just like the ones used to turn the cable cars in the real city. There are some lovely views across the lake by **Lombard's Seafood Grille**, see ⑪③.

The major attraction here is **Disaster! ⑦**, intended to provide an insight into how disaster movies are made. Though it has a corny storyline with Christopher Walken as the demanding director and some hit-and-miss audience participation, the final

Food and Drink ⑪

① FINNEGAN'S BAR AND GRILL
Delancey Street, New York; tel: 407-224-3613; $$
Burgers, chicken, seafood, corned beef, and Irish stew are on the menu, and there's a daily happy hour at Jake and Elwood Blues' favorite watering hole.

② LOUIE'S ITALIAN RESTAURANT
5th Avenue and Canal Street, New York; tel: 407-224-3613; $–$$
A good spot for a break, with Starbucks coffee and a good view of New York. Naturally, pizza and pasta are on the menu indoors.

③ LOMBARD'S SEAFOOD GRILLE
San Francisco/Amity; tel: 407-224-3613; $$
This lakeside restaurant serves the best food in the park. Great clam chowder and seafood dishes, and tasty pastas as well.

disaster sequence aboard a subway train is impressive.

Further on is the quaint Amity set and a gentle boat ride, where lurking round the watery bend is **Jaws** ❽. The mechanical shark is so dated now that it's actually humorous rather than scary, but the suspense of wondering when he'll lunge out of the water is good fun.

Fear Factor Live ❾ is a reality show in which audience participants are chosen in advance. If you have the nerve for it, turn up for casting in front of the stadium about 75 minutes before the show.

WORLD EXPO

Two of the park's biggest attractions are located here. **Men in Black Alien Attack** ❿ is tremendous fun as you ride a spinning car through a darkened city, zapping aliens with your laser gun and racking up points to get your black suit.

Universal Studios' newest attraction is **The Simpsons** ⓫, which opened in spring 2008 and replaced the much-missed Back to the Future ride. Here you join Homer and family on a wild ride through Krusty the Clown's fantasy amusement park, which includes thrill rides, dark rides, and entertainment.

WOODY WOODPECKER'S KIDZONE

This section of the park is filled with diversions for younger visitors, from sing-alongs with Barney to animal shows to playgrounds. A highlight for adults as well is the **E.T. Adventure** ⓬, a charming bicycle ride through the night sky to take E.T. back to his very colorful but ailing planet.

HOLLYWOOD

Sunset Boulevard brings you to the heart of Hollywood, where more tricks of the trade are revealed in the **Universal Horror Make-Up Show** ⓭. It's humorous as well as gruesome. Further down Hollywood Boulevard, **Terminator 2: 3-D** ⓮ uses the original actors in a 3-D film with special effects and live action to continue the story where the movies left off.

On Rodeo Drive, **Lucy – A Tribute** ⓯ honors one of the greatest comediennes of all time, the lovable redhead Lucille Ball.

Above from far left: smiles all round; a kiss from Marilyn; meet Woody; close encounter with Jaws.

VIP Tours
Universal offers personalized VIP tours of one or both parks that take you even deeper behind the scenes. Your guide also takes you straight to the front of the line and directs you to the best seats for rides and attractions. It's a fast and informative way to see the parks. For information tel: 407-363-8295 or email: viptours@universal orlando.com.

Tickets and Information

Universal offers a variety of single-day and multi-day passes to one or both parks. If you plan to see other parks in Orlando as well, a money-saving option is the FlexTicket, which gives you unlimited admission to participating parks for a 14-day period. A five-park FlexTicket covers Universal Studios, Islands of Adventure, SeaWorld, Aquatica, and Wet 'n Wild. The six-park FlexTicket also includes Busch Gardens in Tampa. FlexTickets can be purchased through any participating park. For information and tickets, contact Universal Orlando Resort, 1000 Universal Studios Plaza, Orlando, FL 32819; tel: 407-363-8000; www.universalorlando.com.

6 ISLANDS OF ADVENTURE

From comic book heroes to cartoon classics, fantasy worlds collide here to make a theme park that delights all ages. Among its whimsical backdrops, drenching raft trips and exciting thrill rides, you'll find Orlando's most terrifying roller coasters and its most awesome 3-D adventure.

Above from left:
a hug with Sam-I-Am; Captain America will delight Marvel fans; welcome to the world of Dr Seuss; the Incredible Hulk zooms over Islands of Adventure.

TIME Half to a one day
START Port of Entry
END Seuss Landing
POINTS TO NOTE
Try to get to your top outdoor attractions first, especially in summer when there are often thunderstorms in the afternoon. Park rides will close if lightning is within 5 miles.

Islands of Adventure is set around a small lake, so you can only approach the various islands from one direction or the other. Your actual route will probably depend on whether you have younger children or thrill-seeking teenagers in your party. Although the main focus of this park is on thrilling rides to suit all levels of courage, it also

has shows and some wonderfully creative theme sets to explore. This tour proceeds clockwise around the park, taking in the highlights.

MARVEL SUPER HERO ISLAND

Stroll through the Port of Entry, lined with shops and snack bars. If you need to calm your nerves before or after the rides, try the Backwater Bar at the **Confisco Grille**, see ⑪①, which has a small patio good for people-watching.

When you reach the waterfront, turn left over the bridge and look up – you are now right underneath the first of the park's extreme thrill rides, the **Incredible Hulk Coaster ❶**. This high-speed roller coaster catapults you from 0 to 40 mph (65 kmh) in two sec-

Food and Drink 🍴
① CONFISCO GRILLE
Port of Entry; tel: 407-224-4012; $$
Decked out like an exotic wharfside tavern, this restaurant serves ethnic dishes from fajitas and pad thai to barbecued ribs. Drinks are available at the Backwater Bar, which you can enjoy outdoors on the patio. The restaurant also hosts a character breakfast; phone for days, times, and reservations.

Right:
Spider-Man at Marvel Super Hero Island.

onds, emerging from the starting tube into a zero-gravity roll. It reaches a top speed of 65 mph (100 kmh) and takes you through seven inversions – ie, spins you upside down seven times – and two plunging drops, all in just 2 minutes 15 seconds.

After that, you may think you've lost your senses when you see the likes of Batman and Wonder Woman zooming through the streets, but the superheroes make several appearances throughout the day. There's more spinning and shaking in store at **Storm Force Accelatron ❷** next door, while **Doctor Doom's Fearfall ❸** rockets you 150 feet (45 meters) in the air and

then drops you in stomach-churning intervals to the ground.

The Amazing Adventures of Spider-Man ❹ is the park's most fantastic ride. This high-tech, 3-D experience is a great option for those who want the thrills but don't like roller coasters, although if you suffer from vertigo you might want to think twice.

Outstanding computer animation – seen through your 3-D Spider-Vision glasses – combines with impressive motion simulation as you follow Spider-Man's eerie rooftop journey through the deserted city in search of villains. At one point the superhero jumps right onto your car (sit in front for the

Below:
Hagar the Horrible
in Toon Lagoon.

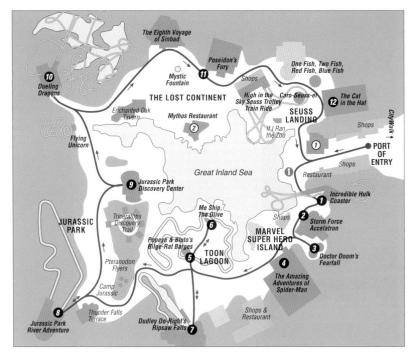

Wizarding World of Harry Potter

Universal scored a coup with Islands of Adventure's newest attraction, The Wizarding World of Harry Potter, scheduled to open in 2009. Set appropriately in the Lost Continent, it will include a re-creation of Hogwart's School, Hogsmeade, and the Forbidden Forest.

best effect) in all his three-dimensional glory. When you take a 40-story plunge from the top of a skyscraper, it all seems terrifyingly real.

TOON LAGOON

As you enter the next island, you feel like you've walked right into the pages of the Sunday funnies. All the classic cartoon characters are here, from Betty Boop to Blondie and Dagwood to Beetle Bailey. The bright colors and larger-than-life whimsical facades add to the sensation of being part of a comic strip.

Ride **Popeye & Bluto's Bilge-Rat Barges ❺** through churning white-water rapids – expect to get soaked. You'll also be fired on by water cannons from **Me Ship, The Olive ❻**, a fun place for young children. More watery thrills are in store at **Dudley Do-Right's Ripsaw Falls ❼**, a flume ride that plunges you down a steep, 75-foot (23-meter) drop at high speed into the pond below – drenching guaranteed.

JURASSIC PARK

If you're still not wet enough, try the **Jurassic Park River Adventure ❽**. After escaping from the claws of giant raptors and the jaws of T-Rex, your boat plunges through the dark to emerge with a big splash in the river below.

This island also contains a kiddie ride and playground, and the **Jurassic Park Discovery Center ❾**, a hands-on interactive attraction where you can scan dinosaur fossils, create a dinosaur with your DNA, and even watch the hatching of a dinosaur egg.

THE LOST CONTINENT

This island of myths and legends contains the park's other mega-roller coaster, **The Dueling Dragons ❿**. It's actually two separate roller coasters – Fire and Ice – which loop and twist like serpents' tails, turning you upside down five times each. Running simultaneously, they come perilously close to

WORLD'S LARGEST

CityWalk

Lining the waterfront between Universal Studios and Islands of Adventure is CityWalk, a dining and nightlife complex with enough themed bars, restaurants, and nightclubs to keep you entertained every night of the week. They include Jimmy Buffett's Margaritaville, the world's largest Hard Rock Café, Pat O'Brien's Orlando (styled after the famous New Orleans original), Bob Marley – A Tribute to Freedom, Nascar Sports Grille, Red Coconut Club, and CityJazz. You can visit CityWalk separately from the parks; there is no admission fee apart from cover charges at some music clubs. It is open from 11am until 2am, and parking is free after 6pm.

each other – within 12–18 inches (30–45cm) – at points during the ride.

There's a tamer roller coaster for younger riders, the Flying Unicorn, and two shows. The Eighth Voyage of Sinbad is a stunt show, while **Poseidon's Fury** ⓫ draws on special effects in an ancient temple, including a walk through an inversion tunnel surrounded by swirling water. Though neither show is great, both have impressive sets. Opposite is the park's best restaurant, **Mythos**, see ⓫②, with great views over the lake.

SEUSS LANDING

The zany world of Dr Seuss comes to life in this wonderful pastel-hued island, one of the most creative sets in any theme park anywhere. The design is so true to the illustrations of the famous children's books that you won't find a single straight line – even the trees are crooked. Although the rides are mostly geared for kids, nostalgic adults love Seuss Landing just as much. Take your time strolling

through here and enjoy all its delightful detail.

Get an overview from the High in the Sky Seuss Trolley Train Ride. Instead of traditional horses, you'll ride Dog-alopes, Cowfish, and Aqua Mop Tops on the Caro-Seuss-el. Steer a fish through squirting musical fountains in One Fish, Two Fish, Red Fish, Blue Fish. The highlight of Seuss Landing is undoubtedly **The Cat in the Hat** ⓬, where you ride through the topsy-turvy household of Dr Seuss' most famous character.

Above from far left: the atmosphere turns giddy in Toon Lagoon; the famous Dueling Dragons; meet Popeye and Olive Oyl.

Below: a scary encounter at the Jurassic Park Discovery Center.

Food and Drink 🍴

② MYTHOS
Lost Continent; tel: 407-224-4012; $$$
The Theme Park Insider Awards gave Mythos the best restaurant award, and with good reason. Its team of chefs prepare innovative dishes – like cedar-planked salmon, balsamic chicken and shrimp primavera – which are a cut above the average theme-park fare. More child-friendly meals are also available. See also p.119.

SEAWORLD AND DISCOVERY COVE

With its fascinating marine animals and spectacular shows, SeaWorld is many people's favorite Orlando park. You can get even closer at its sister park, Discovery Cove, where you can snorkel with the rays and swim with the dolphins.

Buying Tickets

You can save money on your 1-day tickets to SeaWorld by buying them online at home, at least 7 days in advance. Multi-day and multi-park passes, good for one or two years, are also available. SeaWorld is one of the participating parks in the FlexTicket program, which allows unlimited admission to five or six parks for a 14-day period. For information and tickets, contact SeaWorld Orlando, 7007 SeaWorld Drive, Orlando, FL 32821; tel: 407-351-3600 or 1-800-327-2424; www.seaworld.com.

TIME One day for each park
START SeaWorld
END Discovery Cove
POINTS TO NOTE
When you arrive at SeaWorld, take a few minutes to study the schedule of show times. With careful planning you can manage to see all the shows in a single day.

SeaWorld, which opened in 1973, is Florida's best marine park. Like Busch Gardens in Tampa, it is owned and operated by Anheuser Busch. Although it has added a few thrill rides to keep younger visitors happy, the focus of the park is on the animals and the main attractions are its five amazing shows. The animal exhibits – significantly, they're often called 'encounters' – emphasize conservation, information, and awareness as much as entertainment. Most visitors come away much better informed about the marine world.

This, combined with spacious grounds, gives SeaWorld a more relaxed atmosphere than many theme parks. It invites meandering from one animal habitat to another in between shows, and lingering at your favorites. In fact, it's downright hard to tear yourself away from some of them. Unfortunately, there's no way to avoid the long lines for the thrill rides unless you go during one of the main show times.

Be sure to make time for lunch. SeaWorld has the best food of any Orlando theme park, especially in the lower to medium price brackets, and you can enjoy a good selection of Anheuser-Busch beers along with it.

The shows you choose to see and the order in which you see them will determine your route through SeaWorld. This tour describes the highlights, moving in a generally clockwise direction. If this park captures your imagination and your heart, Discovery Cove next door offers an experience that's even more up close and personal.

Food and Drink 🍽

① **CYPRESS BAKERY**
Entrance area, Seaworld; $
Just inside the park gates, this is a good spot to plan your day over coffee, smoothies, mammoth muffins, jumbo cookies, and assorted pastries.

SEAWORLD

Once inside the park entrance, pick up a map and study the show schedule on the back to make sure you don't miss the big productions. The **Cypress Bakery**, see ⓧⓘ, is a good place to have a coffee and plan your day.

Dolphin Cove

Veer left after Turtle Point to watch the playful mammals in **Dolphin Cove ❶**. For a few dollars you can buy some fish at feeding time and stroke the dolphins as you feed them. There is also an underwater viewing

Above from far left: don't miss feeding time; SeaWorld logo; manatees are native to Florida; I spy a killer whale.

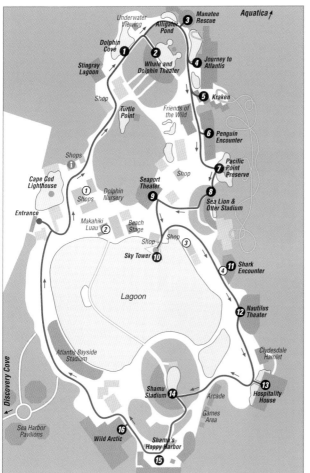

Underwater Viewing
Alligator Pond
❸ Manatee Rescue
Aquatica
Dolphin Cove ❶
❷ Whale and Dolphin Theater
❹ Journey to Atlantis
Stingray Lagoon
Shop
Turtle Point
Friends of the Wild
❺ Kraken
❻ Penguin Encounter
❼ Pacific Point Preserve
Shops
Shop
Cape Cod Lighthouse
ⓘ Shops
Dolphin Nursery
Seaport Theater ❾
❽ Sea Lion & Otter Stadium
Entrance
Makahiki Luau ②
Beach Stage
Shop
Shop ③
Sky Tower ⑩
④ ⑪ Shark Encounter
Lagoon
⑫ Nautilus Theater
Atlantis Bayside Stadium
Clydesdale Hamlet
Discovery Cove
⑬ Hospitality House
Shamu Stadium ⑭
Arcade
Games Area
Sea Harbor Pavilions
⑯ Wild Arctic
Shamu's Happy Harbor
⑮

Winter Wonderland
More than 6,000 pounds (2,700kg) of snow fall every day inside the Penguin Encounter to re-create the birds' Antarctic habitat.

Above: the Whale and Dolphin Theater; prepare to get wet.

area. Nearby at the Stingray Lagoon you can put your hand into the shallow water to feel their smooth skin, but you'll have to be very quick as these fascinating creatures glide swiftly away.

Whale and Dolphin Theater

The **Whale and Dolphin Theater ❷** is the venue for *Blue Horizons*, a colorful show about a young girl who explores the realms of imagination with the dolphin spirit of the sea and the bird spirit of the sky. It combines incredible displays of dolphin jumping, dolphin riding, diving and aerial gymnastics performed by acrobats on trapezes above the water.

Manatee Rescue

Opposite the theater, you can examine two Florida natives, first at the alligator pond and behind it at **Manatee Rescue ❸**. This may be the closest you'll ever come to these elusive and endangered sea mammals. Go down into the underwater viewing area to get a look at their endearing faces.

Thrill Rides

Continue along to the park's two biggest thrill rides. **Journey to Atlantis ❹** is a water coaster ride with a barrage of special effects, drops and dips, ending in a 60-ft (18-meter) soaking plunge that is one of the steepest anywhere. Cobra rolls, vertical loops, and a G-force that keeps you glued to your seat at 65mph (100 kmh) are just a few reasons why **Kraken ❺** is named after mythology's scariest sea monster. This terrifying roller coaster also drenches you in its watery, eel-infested lair.

Below: a sea lion on Pacific Point Preserve.

Food and Drink

② SEAFIRE INN
The Waterfront, SeaWorld; $
Flame-grilled burgers and Sizzlin' Pianos are the top attractions here, with an hourly sing-along between the dueling pianists. Sandwiches and stir-fry are also on the menu.

③ SPICE MILL
The Waterfront, SeaWorld; $
The excellent Caribbean jerk chicken sandwiches and Cajun jambalaya will please those with a spicier palate, and there are milder dishes too. The lakeside deck is a relaxing spot for lunch or just to enjoy a beer and a snack.

Penguin Encounter

Penguin Encounter ❻ is one of the most delightful exhibits in the park. A moving walkway keeps the crowds moving through the long building that houses their icy home. After seeing the puffins in a separate area, you can return to the viewing area above the walkway and watch the penguins to your heart's content. Six species are here, from large king penguins to rockhoppers, and it's fun to watch them waddling over the ice, sliding down the snow mounds, diving and swimming underwater at lightning speed.

Sea Lions and Otters

A walk around **Pacific Point Preserve** ❼, home to sea lions and seals, is also amusing. They're not shy about demanding food with loud, persistent barking. To add to the entertainment, you can buy fish to feed them.

Facing the preserve is the **Sea Lion & Otter Stadium** ❽, where the highly entertaining *Clyde & Seamore Take Pirate Island* show is performed. The sea lions in the starring roles are perfect hams, but the little otter and giant walrus steal several scenes. Get there early to watch the pirate mime warm up the crowd with his hilarious mimicry – stragglers arriving close to showtime may unwittingly become part of his act.

The nearby **Seaport Theater** ❾ is home to a land animal show, *Pets Ahoy*, featuring rescued cats, dogs, pigs and other non-sea critters performing remarkable tricks.

Sky Tower

Stretching along The Waterfront below the **Sky Tower** ❿ (open seasonally; additional charge), a 400-ft (122-meter) observation tower, is a string of shops and restaurants where you'll find a good variety of food and atmosphere. **The Seafire Inn**, see ⑪②, has added lunchtime entertainment with pianos. **The Spice Mill**, see ⑪③, has excellent food and dining on the deck overlooking the lake.

Above from far left: not for the faint-hearted – Kraken; the more gentle appeal of Stingray Lagoon.

Behind the Scenes

Although expensive, these are opportunities to gain privileged access to the sea animals:

Beluga Interaction ($179; two hours; children must be 10 or over). This is a rare chance to get in the water with a Beluga whale. Trainers will teach you a few signals so that you can communicate with these amazing Arctic mammals. Only a few places are available each day.

Marine Mammal Keeper ($399; one day; includes seven-day pass to SeaWorld); children must be 13 or older. This experience takes you backstage to accompany trainers and carers as they prepare meals for SeaWorld's wildlife. You also get up close to the sealife during feeding times.

Sharks Deep Dive ($150; two hours; children must be 10 or over.) This is your chance to get close and personal with the sharks. Participants are locked in a cage and then submerged into an aquarium full of hungry sharks, while being watched by diners at the Underwater Grill restaurant. A special helmet provides air and is equipped with a microphone so you can speak with your cohorts underwater.

Above: an Inca tern at the Discovery Cove aviary; false killer waves perform.

Tickets for Discovery Cove
These can be purchased both with and without the dolphin swim option; daily 9am–5.30pm. Contact Discovery Cove, 6000 Discovery Cove Way, Orlando, FL 32821, tel: 407-370-1280 or 1-877-434-7268; www.discovery cove.com.

Shark Encounter

At the **Shark Encounter** ⓫, these fearsome predators swim around and above you as you walk through a glass tunnel inside the aquarium. This 124-ft (38-meter) tunnel is surrounded by over 450 tons of water – and is strong enough to support the weight of 372 elephants, a total of 2,232 tons. More than 200 species can be seen here and in the open pools outside. Other tanks hold lionfish, eels, barracudas, and other menacing creatures of the deep. You can watch them while you dine at **Sharks Underwater Grill**, see ⓘ⓸.

Nautilus Theater

Graceful acrobats performing amazing feats in a dreamlike, underwater-themed show make *Odyssea* another attraction not to be missed. It is staged in the **Nautilus Theater** ⓬.

Hospitality House

Beyond is the Clydesdale Hamlet, which harbors the brewery's famous horses, and the **Hospitality House** ⓭ where you can get a free sample of the latest Anheuser-Busch brews. You can also sign up for a VIP tasting at the Brewmaster's Club, where you can try a range of beers from lager to stout,

---

Food and Drink 🍴
④ SHARKS UNDER-WATER GRILL
Shark Encounter, SeaWorld; $$$
One entire wall of the restaurant is exposed to the tank. Dine on superb seafood or steak while watching the sharks swim past *(see box p.55)*.

---

learn about how they are brewed, and get tips on the best food to eat with different beers.

Shamu

SeaWorld's star attraction takes place in the **Shamu Stadium** ⓮. The show *Believe* is staged around a magnificent killer whale (in the starring role of Shamu), who leaps out of the water and performs impressive tricks, including drenching the audience in the first 14 rows. Other members of the whale family also get in on the act. Many visitors will find the overly patriotic introduction and the emotional storyline a little hard to take. Put all that aside and just enjoy watching these incredible animals at play. The bond between these whales and their human trainers is truly impressive to see.

The evening Shamu show can be noticeably different than the first afternoon showing, with different members of the whale family taking part. The stadium lights make the atmosphere even more magical too. It's worth seeing the show twice if you can fit everything else in. In the summer months, Shamu Rocks is a nighttime rock 'n' roll concert that combines improvisational 'movements' of the killer whales with music from some of today's hottest stars.

Behind the stadium, **Shamu's Happy Harbor** ⓯ is a play area for kids which also has three kiddie rides. Like its real-world counterpart, **Wild Arctic** ⓰, home to a walrus, entertaining beluga whales and a polar bear, feels quite remote from the rest

of the park. You can also go on a polar expedition via a film and simulated helicopter ride.

DISCOVERY COVE

In a city where it often seems you battle the crowds from breakfast to bedtime, Discovery Cove offers a rare escape. Here admission is limited to 1000 guests a day, ensuring a relaxed, secluded environment where you can interact with wildlife in quiet lagoons.

The highlight is the opportunity to swim with the dolphins. You'll be assigned a time and cabana on arrival, where you meet your trainer before going into the water with a small group. You get to spend about 35–40 minutes with the dolphins, stroking them, learning hand signals to get them to roll and wave, feeding them fish when they respond, and even exchanging kisses. Then you swim out with the trainer and, one by one, the dolphins tow you back to shore.

To swim and play with these beautiful animals is a marvelous experience you'll never forget. You don't have to be a good swimmer to take part. The water isn't deep, and safety vests and wet suits are provided. And park photographers are on hand to capture the thrilling moment.

Discovery Cove offers much more as well. There's a fantastic coral reef where you can snorkel among thousands of tropical fish and large stingrays, and a ray lagoon where you can stroke baby rays. You can float along a warm, lazy river that passes

beneath waterfalls, over submerged ruins, and into an aviary filled with exotic birds of all shapes and sizes. Walk through it and some will even perch on your arm, thanks to the cups of food provided by staff members. You can also just relax in the resort pool or on the sandy beaches.

This priceless experience doesn't come cheap. But everything is included, from towels, lockers and scuba gear to breakfast, all snacks and drinks, and a delicious gourmet lunch. You must book well in advance, because the park is filled to capacity nearly every day. And unless you've a good reason not to, don't forego the dolphin swim – it's a fabulous experience not to be missed.

Above from far left: Shark Encounter aquarium; Shamu says hello; swim with the dolphins at Discovery Cove.

Aquatica

SeaWorld opened its exciting new water park, Aquatica, next door in 2008. True to form, the first slide you come to is the Dolphin Plunge, which shoots you right through a pool of Commerson's dolphins. With their black-and-white markings, they look like miniature killer whales. The park has some killer water slides too, along with a relaxing beach, huge surf pool, a lazy river and colorful kiddie play areas. For more information, see p.68.

8 DOWNTOWN ORLANDO

Downtown Orlando is the heart and soul of the city's arts community. A visit here makes a refreshing change from the theme parks and Disney characters. With a vibrant restaurant and nightlife scene too, this is the perfect Orlando playground for adults.

Wells' Built Museum of African American History
On the west side of I-4, the Wells' Built Museum of African American History (511 W. South Street; tel: 407-245-7535; www.pastinc.org; Mon–Fri 9am–5pm, Sat 10am–2pm; charge) contains memorabilia, photographs and exhibits on the black musicians and artists who entertained in downtown Orlando during the days of segregation. This 1920s hotel housed such notable performers as Ella Fitzgerald and baseball legend Jackie Robinson, and is one of the few lodging stops on the famed Chitlin Circuit still in existence.

DISTANCE 2 miles (3km)
TIME Four to five hours
START Heritage Square
END Thornton Park
POINTS TO NOTE
You may want to time your visit to end with an evening out at Church Street Station, or to take in the Sunday Farmers' Market at Lake Eola.

Theme parks are so dominant in Central Florida that a large number of visitors think Downtown Disney – which is part of Walt Disney World Resort – and Downtown Orlando are one and the same. Even the local taxi drivers often assume that when clients say 'Downtown, please', their destination is Disney. In fact, the two are worlds apart. Make sure to specify Downtown Orlando, and you won't be disappointed.

This tour takes in the most exciting part of the city's commercial center, which spreads north of the international airport and theme parks off I-4. Known as the Downtown Arts District, it encompasses various museums and galleries, theaters and performance venues, Lake Eola Park as well as the trendy Thornton Park neighborhood.

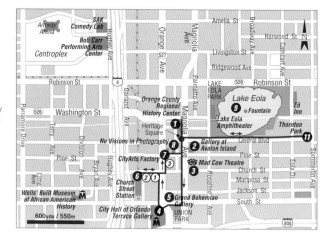

ORANGE COUNTY REGIONAL HISTORY

The tour begins at Heritage Square, a bright modern plaza in the heart of Downtown. Street parking is limited, but a convenient parking garage is located at the southeast corner of the square, at Central Boulevard and Magnolia Avenue opposite the public library. Note that your ticket to the history center includes two hours of free parking here – make sure you validate your parking ticket at the admissions counter.

Bordering the north side of the square you'll find the **Orange County Regional History Center ❶** (65 East Central Boulevard; tel: 407-836-8500; www.thehistorycenter.org; Mon–Sat 10am–5pm, Sun noon–5pm; charge). Constructed in 1927, this Greek Revival building served as the county courthouse until 1999. Now an affiliate of the Smithsonian Institution, the museum houses four floors of interesting exhibits on the history of Orange County.

Starting on the fourth floor, there are displays on Florida's native people, the Seminoles, and the rural pioneers known as 'Crackers'. Note their recipes for baked possum and squirrel soup. Another room devoted to the citrus industry has some great kitschy memorabilia. The third floor takes an entertaining look at the Tin Can Tourists of the 1920s, and a more sobering view of how the coming of Walt Disney World changed Orlando from an agrarian,

citrus-based economy to the tourist mecca it is today.

Across the hall, Courtroom B has been restored to its original state. The first case in the United States in which a conviction was obtained using DNA evidence was tried in this room. Mass murderer Ted Bundy was also tried in the annex, and his name is scratched into the surface of the defense table. On the second floor a glass case holds the original manuscript for Jack Kerouac's *The Dharma Bums*, written on a rented manual typewriter while he was

Above from far left: Orange County Regional History Center; the Seminoles are Florida's native people; old fire engine in Church Street Station.

Below: Bunk Baxter made his name wrestling alligators.

Cultural Corridor
More performance venues lie further north along Downtown Orlando's cultural corridor. On the west side of I-4 are the Bob Carr Performing Arts Center, where Orlando's opera and ballet companies, and philharmonic orchestra perform, the SAK Comedy Lab and the Amway Arena, also the current home of the Orlando Magic basketball team.

Third Thursdays
A good time to visit the Downtown Arts District is on the third Thursday of the month, when the art galleries host an evening Gallery Walk from 6–9pm. Food and drink is often served, and many of the galleries open their new shows on this day.

Below: Downtown Orlando skyline.

living in his mother's back porch apartment in Orlando in 1958.

DOWNTOWN ARTS DISTRICT

From Heritage Square, walk south along Magnolia Avenue. The core of the Downtown Arts District lies along several blocks between here and Orange Avenue. Many of the old storefronts have been brightly painted and renovated to house shops and galleries.

At the corner with Pine Street, the Rogers building is the oldest commercial building in Orlando. It now houses the **Gallery at Avalon Island ❷** (39 S. Magnolia Avenue; tel: 407-803-6670; www.galleryatavalonisland.com; Tue–Sat noon–6pm) and other arts organizations. The gallery features local and international contemporary artists, with new shows opening every month. Further along is the **Mad Cow Theatre ❸** (105 S. Magnolia Avenue; tel: 407-297-8788; www.madcowtheatre. com). This young theater company has won awards for its presentations of classic and contemporary plays and musicals, staged in intimate settings in their two-theater complex. It provides a platform for up-and-coming American talent while staging established theater from around the world.

Turn right on South Street. Walk one block to Orange Avenue and cross the street to the **City Hall of Orlando – Terrace Gallery** ❹ (400 S. Orange Avenue; tel: 407-246-4279; www.city oforlando.net/arts; Mon–Fri 8am–9pm, Sat–Sun noon–5pm). It displays the work of Florida artists and hosts traveling exhibitions throughout the year.

Cross back and walk north along Orange Avenue to reach the entrance to the **Grand Bohemian Gallery** ❺ (325 S. Orange Avenue; tel: 407-581-4801; www.grandbohemiangallery. com; Mon 9.30am–5.30pm, Tue–Sat 9.30am–10pm, Sun 10am–3pm), located in the Grand Bohemian Hotel. This small but superb gallery represents an eclectic range of artists, and is usually full of moneyed clients looking for their next investment.

More artworks are displayed in the hotel reception and bar. Take the elevator to the fifth floor which is a small art museum in itself. In one corridor is a collection of paintings by Marcel Marceau called 'The Third Eye', some featuring his character Bip. Not many people know the famous mime artist was also an accomplished painter. In the business center opposite, there are two paintings by Marc Chagall.

Another corridor is lined with the original paintings by Larry Moore for the playbills for the Orlando Opera. In the Center Gallery are paintings by Dean Cornwell (1892–1960). Called the 'dean of American illustrators', his work appeared in popular magazines like the *Saturday Evening Post* and *Harpers Bazaar*. He also illustrated the works of such authors as Ernest Hemingway and W. Somerset Maugham.

CHURCH STREET STATION

Continue north on Orange Avenue and turn left on Church Street, which leads into **Church Street Station** ❻, a two-block historic district around the old train depot. Most of the buildings date from the 1880s to early 1900s, or have had period architectural features incorporated into their renovation. This was once *the* big nightlife place in Orlando, but it suffered a decline in the 20th century. Now new owners are transforming it into a trendy nightspot once again.

Food and Drink 🍴

① THE DESSERT LADY
120A W. Church Street;
tel: 407-999-5696; $$
Not surprisingly, given the name, dessert is the main course at this divinely decadent dessert and wine café. Bistro lunches, quiches, cheese courses, and tapenades are also served, along with a wide selection of wines, 30 of which are offered by the glass. But the wicked desserts reign and the seductive decor encourages you to indulge.

② CHEYENNE SALOON & OPERA HOUSE
128 W. Church Street; tel: 407-839-3000; Tue–Sat 4pm–2am; $$
This huge drinking and dancing den, lined with golden oak fittings, looks as if it's come straight out of the 1870s. Food is served upstairs, and there's live country & western music on an evening after 8pm, with occasional big-name bands.

Above from far left: the Cheyenne Saloon celebrates the days of the Wild West; old district of Church Street Station.

New Venues
As a stop on the new light rail line which will be built from Sanford to Disney World, Downtown Orlando is set to become a nightlife hotspot in the coming years. Scheduled to open in 2012 at Orange Avenue and South Street is a new performing arts center with three state-of-the-art performance halls. It will host Orlando's philharmonic, ballet and opera companies along with touring Broadway shows. A new Orlando Magic stadium and events center at West Church Street and Hughey Avenue will also be built in the next three years.

A Free Ride
Take a free ride on the circulator bus called LYMMO, which follows a 3-mile (2km) loop around the heart of Downtown Orlando. Catch it at Heritage Square, where it runs along Magnolia Avenue.

Below: cancan dancers at Rosie O'Grady's in Church Street Station.

Outdoor tables are set along the cobbled pavements beneath gleaming wrought-iron galleries. Several high-ceilinged buildings are now home to atmospheric high-concept restaurants such as Ceviche and **The Dessert Lady**, see ⑪① on p.61. Be sure to check out the beautiful golden oak – over a century old – that adorns the bar and balconies of the massive **Cheyenne Saloon & Opera House**, see ⑪② on p.61. Many other restaurants and bars are located in the surrounding streets.

CITYARTS FACTORY

Back on Orange Avenue, walk north past City Plaza, newly developed with a cinema, coffee house and **Bento Café**, a sushi bar, see ⑪③. On the corner of Pine and Orange is the vibrant **CityArts Factory** ❼ (29 S. Orange Avenue; tel: 407-648-7060; www.cityartsfactory.com; Mon–Sat 11am–7pm), set in the former Phillips Theatre built in the 1920s. It serves as a hub for the Downtown Arts District, promoting bohemian as well as upscale artists.

The building now contains a warren of five art galleries, a classroom, and studio space. Upstairs the Eola Capitol Loft is a large open area for hosting performances and events, with an adjacent lounge. The Q Gallery is an upscale visual art gallery with creative, unusual pieces, while at Keila Glassworks you can sometimes see artist Charles Keila at work creating his distinctive vases, plates, and jewelry.

Walk east on Pine Street. About halfway along on the left, a narrow, unobtrusive building houses **Nu Visions in Photography** ❽ (27 E. Pine Street; tel: 407-843-3525; www.nuvisionsin photography.com). The resident photographers renovated a derelict alleyway, closing it in to create the funky, brick-walled gallery. It's open on the third Thursday of the month and for some Friday and Saturday night events, and you can also stop in during the day.

Food and Drink ⑪
③ BENTO CAFÉ
151 S. Orange Avenue; tel: 407-999-8989; $
Sushi is the specialty here, but you can also order noodles and other Asian dishes, Boba tea, and saki. At City Plaza, next to the cinema, this is a good spot for lunch or a light supper.

LAKE EOLA AND THORNTON PARK

Turn left on Magnolia and right on Central Boulevard. This runs along the south side of **Lake Eola** ❾, the site of many city festivals and fireworks displays – this is where the city celebrates 4th July and New Year's Eve. The 43-acre (17-hectare) park is a recreational haven for downtown residents, with a playground, outdoor café, and a 0.9-mile (1.4km) path around the lake for strolling and jogging. You can also cruise the water in swan-shaped paddleboats.

There is an amphitheater for concerts and special events on the west side of the lake, and a variety of shops along Central Boulevard. On Sundays, a farmer's market takes place by the lake's southeast corner at Central and Eola Drive. Local artists also set up tents for the Art Farm, every third Sunday from 10am to 4pm. In November the Fall Fiesta in the Park arts and crafts festival is held here.

Beyond is the old Orlando neighborhood of **Thornton Park** ❿, where new residential lofts and renovated cottages have recently joined the Craftsman-style bungalows and other historic homes. The 1923 Eö Inn overlooks Lake Eola and is now a boutique hotel with a spa *(see p.112)*. A string of trendy restaurants, bars, and shops line the main crossroads of Central Boulevard and Summerlin Avenue, making this a chic spot in the city for drinking and dining.

(see p.112)

Above from far left: Thornton Park shops; world-class artists feature at the Grand Bohemian Gallery; flying the flag; the American way.

Shakespeare in the Park
Lake Eola's amphitheater lends itself beautifully to Shakespeare; the Orlando Shakespeare Theater hopes to be resuming performances here in 2009. For more information, contact www.orlandoshakes.org.

Left: Swan boats on Lake Eola.

9

LOCH HAVEN PARK

Downtown Orlando's cultural corridor continues three miles (5km) north in Loch Haven Park, an enclave of outstanding museums and performing arts venues separated from the surrounding streets by verdant grounds. Nearby are the lush landscapes of the Harry P. Leu Gardens.

Where to Park

The Orlando Museum of Art has a large parking lot behind the building, which also serves the theaters. You can walk to the Science Center from there. Alternatively, there are a limited number of parking spaces in front of the Mennello Museum of American Art, and a large parking garage opposite the Science Center, which is a short walk away.

DISTANCE 2 miles (3km)

TIME Half a day

START Orlando Museum of Art

END Harry P. Leu Gardens

POINTS TO NOTE

Apart from the café inside the Science Center, there are no restaurants in or near Loch Haven Park, so make sure you bring some snacks if you plan to spend a long time in the museums or at Leu Gardens.

Set between three lakes, Loch Haven Park contains 45 acres (18 hectares) devoted to art and culture. And with the excellent Orlando Science Center, there's enough to fascinate children as well as adults.

ORLANDO MUSEUM OF ART

Housed in a handsome circular building, the **Orlando Museum of Art ❶** (2416 N. Mills Avenue; tel: 407-896-4231; www.OMArt.org; Tue–Fri 10am–4pm, Sat–Sun noon–4pm;

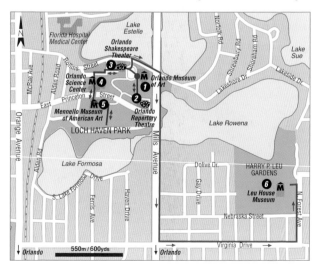

charge) stages big touring exhibitions every two years in addition to those from its permanent collection of American, African and ancient Hispanic art.

A towering glass sculpture by Dale Chihuly stands in the atrium at the entrance to the galleries. To the left is the Lakeview Promenade Gallery, lined with intriguing portraits in a variety of mediums, and a gallery of African Art with themed exhibitions ranging from textiles to vessels. This leads into the Art of the Ancient Americas gallery, with a fascinating collection of ceramic vessels and figures, gold jewelry, copper figurines, masks, tiny carved beads as well as decorative and ritual objects from Central and South America dating back to 2000 BC.

The galleries to the right of the atrium contain a rotating collection of American art from the 18th century to the present, including landscapes, portraits, and traditional and contemporary sculpture. The museum's permanent collection includes works by Georgia O'Keeffe, John James Audubon, John Singer Sargent, and several American Impressionist painters.

ORLANDO THEATERS

Next to the art museum is the **Orlando Repertory Theatre ❷** (1001 E. Princeton Street; tel: 407-896-7365; www.orlandorep.com), a family-oriented professional theater company whose productions are based on classic and contemporary children's literature.

Across the parking lot you'll find a domed building housing the **Orlando Shakespeare Theater ❸** (812 E. Rollins Street; tel: 407-447-1700; www.orlandoshakes.org), which stages the Bard's classics as well as contemporary plays. It is also one of the main venues for the Orlando Fringe Festival *(see box, p.67)*.

ORLANDO SCIENCE CENTER

A path beside the theater leads to the **Orlando Science Center ❹** (777 E. Princeton Street; tel: 407-514-2000, www.osc.org; Mon–Thur 10am–6pm, Fri–Sat 10am–9pm; charge). It contains a giant CineDome movie theater and an observatory, plus dozens of hands-on exhibits spread over four levels.

The exhibits appeal mainly to children of varying ages. Among the highlights are the dinosaurs on Level 4 and the robots on Level 2. The Nature Works exhibit on Level 1 has a pond with turtles and alligators, while in the Trading Center kids can get a close-up view of tarantulas, giant millipedes and other creepy creatures.

Above from far left: Orlando Museum of Art; a painting by Earl Cunningham at the Mennello Museum; celebrating Florida's favorite fruit.

Above: a colorful Dale Chihuly exhibit at the Orlando Museum of Art.

Food and Drink 🍴

Unfortunately Loch Haven Park lacks any restaurants or cafés, and there are none in the nearby streets. The only option for refreshment is to bring your own or try the café at the Science Center, which has a variety of food selections. There are also vending machines at Harry P. Leu Gardens.

OF AMERICAN ART

Family Treasures
Among the interesting artifacts in the Leu House Museum are a mourning wreath made of human hair, a top hat made of beaver fur, a spool bed, an Oliver type-writer (predecessor to the Olivetti), and a morning glory gramo-phone that still plays.

Below: exotic plant at Leu Gardens.

MENNELLO MUSEUM OF AMERICAN ART

For a safe way across the busy road, take the pedestrian bridge from the Science Center to the parking garage. From here it's a short walk to the **Mennello Museum of American Art** ❺ (900 E. Princeton Street; tel: 407-246-4278; www.mennellomuseum.org; Tue–Sat 10.30am–4.30pm, Sun noon–4.30; charge).

This small but important museum is based around the paintings of Earl Cunningham, a self-taught artist who has been called one of the most innovative landscape painters of his generation. His bright palette and energetic scenes of forests and coast-lines are full of life and well-observed detail, while his tiny, exquisitely rendered birds and people are reminiscent of L.S. Lowry.

The museum has a small room of American folk art, featuring carved wooden sculptures, pottery, paintings and other works by Hispanic and African-American artists. It also stages temporary exibitions. Outside, be sure to see the amazing Southern Live Oak, called the 'Old Mayor', opposite the entrance by the parking area. Over 550 years old, its enormous branches are so heavy they touch the ground. Then take a stroll through the sculpture garden in the grounds beside the lake.

LEU GARDENS

To visit some of Central Florida's finest gardens, you'll have to return to your car. The route is well signposted. Depending on where you've parked, drive southeast on E. Princeton Street to the end of Loch Haven Park and turn right on N. Mills Avenue. (If

you're parked behind the Orlando Art Museum, exit by the museum and turn right directly onto N. Mills.) Then turn left at Virginia Drive and after about half a mile (800 meters), make a slight left at N. Forest Avenue, then turn left to stay on N. Forest.

The entrance to the **Harry P. Leu Gardens** ❻ (1920 N. Forest Avenue; tel: 407-246-2620; www.leugardens.org; daily 9am–5pm; charge) is just beyond. Encompassing nearly 50 acres (20 hectares) on the shores of Lake Rowena, it contains a stunning array of features including a native wetland garden, tropical stream garden, desert garden, herb, vegetable and citrus gardens, and the largest formal rose garden in Florida.

Leu Gardens is most famous for its camellias. With more than 2,000 specimens, it is the largest documented collection in eastern North America. Spread out beneath mature oaks in the North and South Woods, they bloom from October through March. From the boardwalk overlooking the lake, you can see alligators, heron, and a variety of shorebirds.

In the center of the grounds is the **Leu House Museum** (museum tours 10am–3.30pm, closed in July). Dating from 1888, and filled with fine period furniture and household items, it offers an intriguing look at the Central Florida lifestyle through the four families who owned it. The property was purchased in 1936 by Harry P. Leu, a rich businessman, and he and his wife developed the gardens, donating it to the city in 1961.

With extensive grounds and so many fascinating gardens to explore, it's hard to make a quick visit here. You could easily spend several hours, depending on your interests. The last admission time is 4pm.

Above from far left: Mennello Museum of American Art; the flowers on display at Leu Gardens are stunning.

Orlando Fringe Festival

This 12-day festival takes over Loch Haven Park around the last two weeks of May every year, and is the longest-running of all the fringe festivals in the US. It aims to provide an accessible, affordable outlet for theater, music, dance, art and madness of all types. Nightly concerts are held on an outdoor stage and performances also take place at the Orlando Shakespeare Theater. The Kids Fringe puts on around 45 child-friendly shows.

Performers come in all shapes and sizes from all over the world, and you never know quite what to expect; you may get amateurs struggling with first-time nerves, or you may see the next big thing – it's all part of the fun. Imagine the Edinburgh Fringe except with guaranteed sunshine. For more information, contact: www.orlandofringe.org.

10

INTERNATIONAL DRIVE

Love it or hate it, I-Drive is one of Orlando's most important tourist thoroughfares. Along this wide boulevard you'll find theme parks, water parks, attractions, dinner shows, discount outlets, malls and a host of shops and restaurants catering for every taste and budget.

I-Ride Trolley

Skip the traffic and do I-Drive on the I-Ride Trolley. It runs daily from 8am to 10pm, with stops at over 100 locations roughly every 20 minutes. Single fares are $1, kids age 12 and under ride free with adults. There are also unlimited ride passes ranging from one day ($3) to 14 days ($16). Passes are sold at many locations around the city. For more information tel: 407-354-5656; www.IRideTrolley.com

> **DISTANCE** 9 miles (14km)
> **TIME** Thirty minutes to drive plus sightseeing and shopping time
> **START** Vineland Avenue
> **END** Oakridge Road
> **POINTS TO NOTE**
> The area around the Convention Center can become hopelessly jammed when a big show is in town. Allow extra time, or avoid it altogether during peak times.

International Drive rivals US 192 in Kissimmee as the area's most tourist-oriented stretch of road. This isn't surprising, as it serves the visitor vortex of the Orange County Convention Center. You'll find I-Drive, as it's commonly called, alternately smart or somewhat tacky, depending on the hotels, shops, and attractions along any given stretch.

Although I-Drive's southern boundary is Highway 192, there is nothing much of interest except more hotels and open spaces waiting to be developed until you reach Vineland Avenue, where our tour begins. It is anchored at either end by two of the city's largest designer outlet malls, so plan to bag some bargains on this route.

If you're coming from I-4, take exit 68 east to reach **Orlando Premium Outlets** ❶ (8200 Vineland Avenue; tel: 407-238-7787; www.premium outlets.com; Mon–Sat 10am–11pm, Sun 10am–9pm). Set around an interior open-air court, it features such designer names as Armani, Ralph Lauren, Salvatore Ferragamo, and Calvin Klein among its 110 stores, plus a Barneys New York outlet.

From the mall, drive north on I-Drive. Central Florida Parkway divides SeaWorld from its sister park, Discovery Cove *(see p.57)*. Next door to SeaWorld is Orlando's newest attraction, **Aquatica** ❷ (5800 Water Play Way; tel: 888-800-5447; www.aquatica byseaworld.com; hours vary by season; charge), opened in spring 2008. This fantastic water park, operated by Sea-World, has a South Seas Island-style

> ### Food and Drink 🍴
> ① **TOMMY BAHAMA'S TROPICAL CAFÉ AND EMPORIUM**
> 9101 International Drive at Pointe Orlando; tel: 321-281-5888; $$
> Delicious island-inspired food. Enjoy a light lunch or dessert on the terrace after shopping or relax in the Bungalow Bar. Dinner entrées are superb.

theme with highlights including 36 waterslides, side-by-side wave pools, animal encounters and white sand beaches. Aquatica's signature attraction is the Dolphin Plunge, a 300-ft (90-meter) waterslide which takes a 42-ft (13-meter) drop and plunges riders into a crystal-clear lagoon full of black-and-white Commerson's dolphins.

BEACHLINE EXPRESSWAY TO SAND LAKE ROAD

Cross under 528, the airport toll road also known as the Beachline Expressway. The nicest stretch of I-Drive runs between here and Sand Lake Road, along a wide landscaped boulevard.

The road curves west between the massive south and west concourses of the **Orange County Convention Center** ❸ (9899 and 9800 International Drive; tel: 407-685-1061). With more than 2.1 million square feet (200,000 square meters), it is ranked second in the country for exhibition space after Chicago's convention center.

On the right, wedged between I-Drive and Universal Boulevard, is **Pointe Orlando** ❹ (9101 International Blvd; tel: 407-248-2838; www.pointe orlando.com; daily from 10am), a smart shopping and dining center with favorites like **Tommy Bahama's Tropical Café and Emporium**, see ⑪①, where you can shop and eat island-style. Valet parking is free in the evenings for the restaurants.

The upside-down building alongside is **WonderWorks** ❺ (9067 International Drive; tel: 407-351-8800;

www.wonderworksonline.com; daily 9am–midnight; charge), a wacky world of optical illusions, tricks and interactive exhibits spread over four floors. It's not as shiny (nor as expensive) as the theme parks, but it's good fun for adults as well as kids, with an inversion tunnel, bed of nails, and many other amusing exhibits.

Above from far left: one of many sports emporiums on I-Drive; the FAO Schwartz toy store; Tiki Island Adventure Golf recreates a Pacific Island theme; the upside-down WonderWorks.

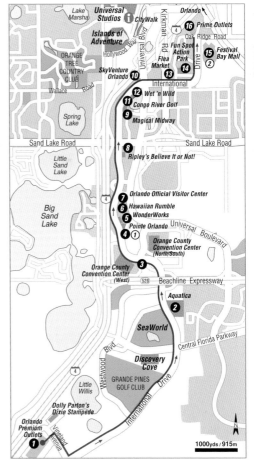

I-Drive Dinner Shows

A number of the popular dinner shows (see p.17) are located along or just off I-Drive. These include Dolly Parton's Dixie Stampede, the Outta Control Magic Comedy Dinner Show, Tony n' Tina's Wedding, Sleuth's Mystery Dinner Show and Pirate's Dinner Adventure. Details are available from the Visitor Center.

Play a round of miniature golf in an island-themed setting next door at **Hawaiian Rumble** ❻ (8969 International Drive; tel: 407-351-7733; www.hawaiianrumbleorlando.com; charge).

Set back off the road beside Austrian Row is the **Orlando Official Visitor Center** ❼ (8723 International Drive; tel: 407-363-5872; www.orlandoinfo.com; daily 8.30am–6.30pm). You can pick up free maps, visitor guides, brochures and discount coupons to restaurants and attractions; buy tickets for the theme parks and I-Ride Trolley, and get directions. Helpful staff are on hand to answer questions and help with finding last-minute accommodations.

Further on the right, a tilting building holds the Orlando branch of the famed **Ripley's Believe It or Not!** ❽ (8201 International Drive; tel: 407-363 4418; www.ripleysorlando.com; daily 9am–1am; charge). This aptly named Odditorium is filled with bizarre exhibits collected by writer and cartoonist Robert Ripley, who traveled the world in the 1920s–1940s. A lot of the displays seem dated today – animal and human deformities, tribal adornments and the like no longer seem shocking in our

world of high-tech special effects. Still, there are some curiosities to be found among the more dubious displays.

NORTH OF SAND LAKE ROAD

The next stretch of I-Drive is characterized by a string of budget hotels, restaurants, and discount outlets. The mile after that offers many options for thrill-seekers. **Magical Midway** ❾ (7001 International Drive; tel: 407-370-5353; www.magicalmidway.com) has elevated go-kart tracks, classic midway rides, a video arcade, and the Slingshot bungee jump and Star Flyer tower rides.

Further along, on a side road to the left, **SkyVenture Orlando** ❿ (6805 Visitors Circle; tel: 407-903-1150; www.skyventureorlando.com) is an indoor skydiving experience where you float on a column of air in a vertical wind tunnel.

For a tamer adventure, try **Congo River Golf** ⓫ (6312 International Drive; tel: 407-352-0042; www.congoriver.com), a tropical-themed miniature golf course with waterfalls, caves, and live alligators. A second location is further along on I-Drive.

Right: The Flyer offers Wet 'n Wild's biggest thrills.

Wet 'n Wild ⑫ (6200 International Drive; tel: 407-351 9453; www.wetnwildorlando.com; hours vary; charge) was the world's first water park, opened in 1977. It's still one of the most exciting, with thrill rides such as Brain Wash, a 60-foot (18-meter) plunge through a mind-numbing funnel, and the Storm, where you drop through an elevated chute that sends you spinning into a giant bowl below. Several multi-person rides add to the high-octane thrills. The Kids' Park has miniature versions of the favorite rides, and the park is open year-round with heated pools during the cooler months.

Turn left on Universal Boulevard for Universal Studios *(see p.44)*, Islands of Adventure *(see p.48)* and CityWalk *(see p.50)*. Or carry on along I-Drive into a world of shopping.

On your left is the **International Drive Flea Market** ⑬ (5545 International Drive; tel: 407-352-2525; daily 10am–8pm), with 300 booths selling everything from clothing, jewelry, and electronics to souvenirs. Behind are more rides and arcade games at **Fun Spot Action Park** ⑭ (5551 DelVerdeWay; tel: 407-363-3867; www.fun-spot.com).

The huge **Festival Bay Mall** ⑮ (5250 International Drive; tel: 407-351-7718; www.shopfestivalbaymall.com; Mon–Sat 10am–9pm, Sun 11am–7pm) sprawls on the right side of the road, with Sheplers Western Wear, Bass Pro Shops Outdoor World, and a Ron Jon Surfpark. Eat at the **Cricketeers Arms English Pub & Eatery**, see ⑪②.

International Drive ends at Oakridge Road. Straight ahead is Orlando's largest outlet mall, **Prime Outlets** ⑯ (5401 W. Oakridge Road; tel: 407-352-9600; www.primeoutlets.com; daily 10am–9pm). All the top brand names are here, along with designer outlets for Calvin Klein, Geoffrey Beene, Ann Taylor, and a Neiman Marcus Last Call.

Above from far left: enjoy a juicy steak at Wild Jack's; busy I-Drive; cooling off in Wet 'n Wild.

Minimum Height
For most of the serious thrill rides in Wet 'n Wild, riders have to be at least 48" (122cm) tall. In the Kids' Park, that is the maximum height for most of the rides.

Ripley's World

Robert Ripley (1890–1949) drew a daily cartoon feature which was published in over 40 countries. He traveled extensively, visiting 198 countries over a period of 30 years (his favorite being China), and began bringing back his finds because his critics called him a liar. His first Believe It or Not book of facts, published in 1929, was on the bestseller list for months. If all his books ever sold were stacked on top of each other, they would reach over 100 times the height of the Empire State Building.

Food and Drink 🍴
② CRICKETEERS ARMS ENGLISH PUB & EATERY
Festival Bay Mall; tel: 407-354-0686; $
A little piece of England in the heart of Orlando, serving fish and chips, bangers and mash, and other pub stalwarts from across the pond. Choose from 17 tap beers including 4 hand-drawn ales.

KISSIMMEE AND CELEBRATION

With its low-cost hotels and proximity to Disney World, Kissimmee is the base for many visitors. The minor attractions here provide some entertainment between visits to the big theme parks and offer a glimpse of the region in the days before Disney.

Driving Tips

Watch for the brightly colored Guide Markers along West US 192, which will help you locate hotels and attractions. If you're staying in the central or eastern part of Kissimmee, the Osceola Parkway (Toll Road 522) leads directly into Walt Disney World Resort. It's worth the toll to avoid the traffic on US 192 and I-4.

DISTANCE 57 miles (92km)
TIME One to two days
START Celebration
END Cypress Gardens
POINTS TO NOTE
Because of its proximity to Walt Disney World, US 192 is almost always busy, especially the nearer you get to I-4, so allow extra time to reach your destination. Historic Downtown Kissimmee shuts up shop by 3pm on Saturdays.

South of the city limits and adjacent to Disney World, Kissimmee blends seamlessly into Orlando. It sprawls along US 192, also known as the Irlo Bronson Memorial Highway, one of the area's main tourist drags. Lined with more chain hotels, restaurants and gaudy souvenir shops than you can count, this busy road also serves the clusters of vacation homes, most of which are centered in the vicinity.

Kissimmee grew up as a center for the region's ranchers and farmers, offering a bit of fun for the family

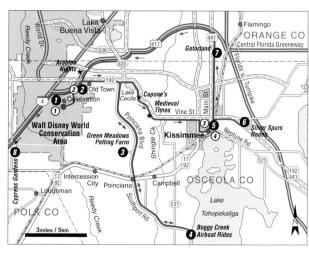

when they came to town for the cattle market or rodeo. Although those days are rapidly disappearing, you'll still see cattle grazing alongside new holiday home developments just a couple of miles south of town. This tour travels east from I-4, where Kissimmee's historic downtown, rodeo grounds and Lake Toho are a reminder of the region's rural roots.

CELEBRATION

First, however, make a detour to Disney's model town of **Celebration ❶**, a place where small-town idealism meets New Urbanism. Walt Disney was fascinated with the idea of building a town that would foster community life and environmental principals using the latest technological advances. He thought about every aspect of town planning, from schools to waste disposal to layouts that would encourage neighborly interaction.

Celebration was based on Disney's model for a town, but construction didn't start until 1994, nearly 30 years after his death. Though it was laid out on land owned by the company, contrary to popular belief, it was not built for Disney employees. The first residents were chosen by lottery. In the early phases, each house was different, based on vernacular styles from across the country. The result is a bright, shiny, neat-as-a-pin town. The attention to detail and well-conceived planning makes a welcome relief from the brash anarchy of both US 192 and International Drive, where the only

driving tenet behind construction seems to be bigger, better, louder.

From Highway 192, turn south on Celebration Avenue (from I-4, take exit 62 and turn left onto Celebration Boulevard) and follow signs to Market Street. This is the heart of town, curving prettily around a small lake. It's a pleasant place to stroll, browse in the shops, or have a coffee or bite to eat in one of several good restaurants. The **Market Street Café**, see ⓌⓉ, has a lakeside view.

Several top architects were hired to design the community buildings. At the top of Market Street is Charles Moore's Preview Center, the town's tallest building (Bank of America now occupies the ground floor). It recalls the storm lookout towers used to mark new real estate developments in Florida's early 'wildcat' days.

Opposite is the red-brick town hall with its 52 white columns, designed by Philip Johnson. Next door, postmodernist architect Michael Graves designed the post office with outdoor mailboxes to facilitate contact among residents. Down by the lake, the twin spires of Cesar Pelli's cinema soar above the playful interactive fountain.

Above from far left: classic cars line up along Trophy Row; characterful sign in Old Town.

Above: Celebration's logo; recommended Market Street Café in the town center.

Food and Drink Ⓦ
① MARKET STREET CAFÉ

Market Street, Celebration;
tel: 407-566-1144; $–$$
This café offers freshly made diner-style dishes from pecan pancakes to pork chop dinners, and treats from the soda fountain. There's also outdoor seating with views of the lake.

Headwaters of the Everglades

Lake Toho is part of the Kissimmee chain of lakes, which forms the headwaters to the Florida Everglades. Water runs from these lakes via creeks, levees and the Kissimmee River to Lake Okeechobee, the start of the Everglades watershed. A $7.8 billion restoration is underway along the river to help save the Everglades, an ecosystem unique in tho world.

OLD TOWN

Returning to reality on US 192 comes as quite a shock after even a short time in Celebration. Luckily **Old Town ❷** (5770 W. Hwy 192; www.old-town. com; 10am–11pm) is just down the road. To put it in movie terms, it's like going from *The Truman Show* to *Happy Days*.

Not to be confused with downtown Kissimmee, Old Town is a shopping, dining and entertainment attraction that harks back to the 1950s. Its main street is lined with specialty shops and amusements that appeal mainly to kids and teenagers, such as the Haunted Grimm House. But with '50s tunes setting the mood, and beautiful old cars stationed at the corners, adults enjoy strolling along the shaded arcades, perhaps with a stick of cotton candy or a root beer from **A&W**, see ①②, for old times' sake.

Anchoring Old Town at one end are several thrill rides, including the V-shaped towers of the Sling Shot, visible for miles. At the other end are traditional fairground rides and midway games. More thrills are right next door at Fun Spot, with a race track, bumper cars and a scary bungee jump attraction.

Food and Drink 🍽

② A&W ALL AMERICAN FOOD
Old Town; tel: 407-397-2280; $
Burgers, fries and of course root beer at this Old Town branch of America's favorite drive-in.

The highlight is the Saturday Nite Cruise, when a parade of classic cars motors through Old Town (there's a Friday Nite Cruise too, for 'newer' cars from 1975 and up). People set up lawn chairs along the street to watch the cruise, which begins at 8.30pm. A live band plays '50s and '60s music until 11pm.

On cruise days the automobiles are lined up on display along Trophy Row from late morning on. Even if you're not that keen on cars, the shiny paintwork, chrome and interiors of classic models in immaculate condition is impressive to see.

PETTING FARM

Just off US 192 is Lake Tohopekaliga. Since few can pronounce its Indian name, which means 'sleeping cat', it's better known as Lake Toho. There's no better way to explore it than from the water on a traditional Florida means of transport, an airboat.

Turn right on Poinciana Boulevard, which runs south out of the city. If you have small children you may want to make a detour on the way to **Green Meadows Petting Farm ❸** (1368 S. Poinciana Boulevard; tel: 407-846-0770; www.greenmeadowsfarm.com; 9.30am–5.30pm; charge), where they can milk a cow, have a pony ride and other activities on a two-hour tour.

AIRBOAT RIDES

It's a 19-mile (30-km) drive from US 192 to the southwest shore of the

lake. Poinciana Boulevard eventually becomes Southport Road, which leads to Southport Park, the peaceful location of **Boggy Creek Airboat Rides** ❹ (2001 E. Southport Road; tel: 407-344-9550; www.bcairboats.com; daily 9am–5.30pm; charge). No reservations are needed for the 30-minute rides, which run continuously throughout the day. You can also book longer private tours, and night tours (April–October).

Airboats are a thrilling way to experience the natural environment of the Central Florida Everglades. Piloted by Master Captains, they glide over the shallow surface of the lake, reaching speeds of more than 50 mph (80 kmh), or putter beside grassy hammocks and into narrow, swampy glades between the cypress trees in search of wildlife.

Alligators are the prime animal everyone comes to see, but these wetlands also harbor turtles, snakes, bald eagles, osprey, rare snail kites, pelicans, sandhill cranes and a host of migrating birds. March to May is the best time for wildlife, while on the night tours you hunt for alligators who in turn are hunting their prey.

HISTORIC DOWNTOWN KISSIMMEE

Return to US 192 by the same route and turn right to continue the tour. Fans of roadside Americana are in for a treat. Kissimmee has some of the best kitsch storefronts in the country. Look for the citrus market shaped like a giant orange, aptly named Orange World, and enormous mermaids, wiz-

Above from far left: the best way to see the wildlife; airboat driver; you should see herons and alligators in the Everglades.

Below: airboat rides are a popular way to explore the wetlands.

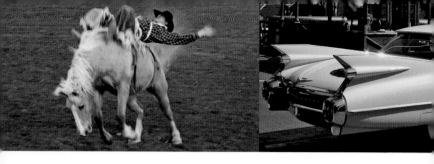

Dinner Shows

Kissimmee also has its share of popular dinner shows located along US 192. These include Arabian Nights, Capone's and Medieval Times.

Rodeo Day

February's rodeo weekend is a long-time tradition in Osceola County, and students get an official day off school to celebrate Friday's opening day.

ards, alligators and the like beckoning you in to souvenir shops, mini-golf and attractions. There's also a sprinkling of English-style pubs, such as the **Fox & Hounds**, see ⑪③.

Watch for brown signs directing you to Kissimmee's historic district. Turn right on John Young Boulevard, then left on Emmett Street which brings through a pretty old residential neighborhood before swinging left onto Broadway. This is the start of **Historic Downtown Kissimmee ❺**.

There's not a lot to see besides a few antiques shops, lakefront park and a farmers' market on Thursdays (7am–1pm), but the old storefronts are attractive, especially along Broadway. Look for the mural on the hardware store depicting the town's rural days.

Joanie's Diner, see ⑪④, is a good place to stop for refreshments.

SILVER SPURS RODEO

Continue north on Main Street back to US 192. If the rodeo is in town, turn right to reach Osceola Heritage Park, home of the Silver Spurs Arena. Twice a year in February and June, Kissimmee hosts the **Silver Spurs Rodeo ❻** (tel: 407-677-6336; www.silverspursrodeo.com; charge), the largest rodeo east of the Mississippi.

Professional riders compete in events such as bull riding, steer wrestling and barrel racing over three days. There are rodeo clowns, rodeo queens and displays of horsemanship that celebrate the area's long cattle ranching heritage.

Right: getting close and personal at Gatorland.

GATORLAND

Take Main Street north of US 192 and it becomes the Orange Blossom Trail, leading to one of Orlando's oldest attractions. **Gatorland** ❼ (14501 South Orange Blossom Trail; tel: 407-855-5496; www.gatorland.com; daily 9am–5pm; charge) was started in 1949 by Kissimmee cattle rancher Owen Godwin. It's a combination theme park and working gator farm which breeds the animals for their meat and hides. It also works with the University of Florida on alligator research and promotes a conservation message.

Classic attractions here include the Gator Jumparoo show, where the enormous reptiles leap out of the water to grab their dinner, and the Gator Wrestling show. There are also displays of deadly snakes and other wildlife, eco-tours and the Gator Gully Splash Park.

CYPRESS GARDENS

Florida's oldest theme park lies about 40 miles south of Kissimmee in Winter Haven. Take the Highway 417 toll road (just north of Gatorland) west to I-4, then take I-4 West to US 27 South (exit 55). Turn right on State Road 540/Cypress Gardens Boulevard. The park is 4 miles (6.5km) on the left.

Cypress Gardens ❽ (6000 Cypress Gardens Boulevard; tel: 863-324-2111; www.cypressgardens.com; hours vary by season, open from 10am; charge) has had to compete with the big theme parks over the years by adding 40 rides and a water park. But the main reason to visit is the same as it's always been: the beautiful gardens. Among the highlights are the Topiary Trail, where Southern belles stroll among huge, whimsical topiary creations, and the extensive Botanical Gardens that wind along the lake shore surrounding an enormous Banyan tree.

The park has been staging water ski shows since 1936, and the champion ski team is one of the best around. It's well worth catching this impressive display of ski jumping, barefoot skiing, acrobatics, team jumping and free flying. Although the jokes are a bit corny at times, the show is a real gem of Americana.

Cypress Gardens also has an impressive line-up of big-name stars in nighttime concerts throughout the year. Concerts are free with park admission, so check the schedule and time your visit accordingly.

Above from far left: Silver Spurs Rodeo, Kissimmee; one of many classic cars in Old Town; old-fashioned big wheel.

Above: creativity at Cypress Gardens.

Food and Drink 🍴

③ FOX & HOUNDS PUB
3514 W. Vine Street (US 192); tel: 407-847-9927; $
The Fox & Hounds is the place to catch the latest football (soccer) match while enjoying British ales, lager, cider and pub grub from fish and chips to shepherd's pie.

④ JOANIE'S DINER
120 Broadway; tel: 407-933-0519; $
Locals meet at Joanie's for the winning combination of down-home food and warm, convivial atmosphere. A good choice for an inexpensive breakfast, lunch or dinner.

WINTER PARK

Although it lies just north of downtown Orlando, Winter Park seems a world away from the theme parks and commercial center. With its oak-lined brick streets, upscale shops and restaurants and handsome old neighborhoods, it's a refreshing change of pace from the tourist-oriented city.

Above: artwork from the Morse Museum of American Art.

DISTANCE 2½ miles (4km)
TIME Three hours plus museum/shopping time
START Morse Museum
END Cornell Fine Arts Museum
POINTS TO NOTE
The museums close Mondays. There is a North and South Park Avenue, which divides at Morse Boulevard.

Surrounded by large lakes, Winter Park was founded in 1881 as a winter resort for northerners. The Amtrak station and railroad tracks running through the heart of town are reminders that these early, wealthy visitors came by train.

As the citrus-growing business thrived, so did the town, and Winter Park developed a lifestyle of gracious homes and fine cultural institutions that remains today. Rollins College, an elite, private institution named for one of the city founders, is among the top-rated liberal arts colleges in the country.

In a world of ever-increasing chains, Winter Park stands out for its high-quality, one-off shops and restaurants. Park Avenue, the main thoroughfare, has around 140 stores and galleries, as well as cafés, bars, and fine dining.

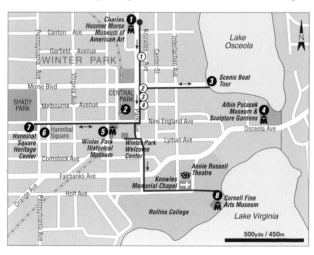

CHARLES HOSMER MORSE MUSEUM OF AMERICAN ART

The tour begins at the **Charles Hosmer Morse Museum of American Art ❶** (445 N. Park Avenue; tel: 407-645-5311; www.morsemuseum.org; Tue–Sat 9.30am–4pm, Sun 1–4pm; charge). From lamps and leaded-glass windows to pottery, jewelry, paintings and art glass, it contains the world's most comprehensive collection of works by Louis Comfort Tiffany (1848–1933). Also on display is an important collection of American art pottery.

A highlight is the Tiffany Chapel, designed by the artist himself for the World's Columbian Exposition in Chicago in 1893. The Byzantine-style interior with its carved arches and intricate glass mosaics covering every inch of the pillars, altar, and baptismal font is simply stunning, while an enormous cross-shaped electrified chandelier hangs overhead.

PARK AVENUE

Stroll south along Park Avenue. The eclectic range of stores and galleries is an invitation to browsing and window-shopping. A few to watch for include Timothy's Gallery (No. 236), a top-rated gallery of American crafts; Bullfish (No. 102), a pet boutique, wine, and gourmet store; and Ten Thousand Village (No. 346) with fairly traded handicrafts from all around the world.

A good place to fortify yourself with a coffee or ice cream is at the **Briarpatch Restaurant**, see ❶①, where tables with bright yellow umbrellas are set out beneath the beautiful oaks draped in Spanish moss.

Park Avenue is often said to have a European style, with its cobbled street, sidewalk tables and restaurants like **Bosphorus**, see ❶②, which serves Turkish cuisine. But many of its two-story buildings look right out of 1920s America. Just south of Bosphorus is **Barnie's Coffee and Tea Company**, see ❶③, and further along, the **Eola Wine Company**, see ❶④, is a distinctly local enterprise *(see p.81)*.

On the opposite side of the street, shady **Central Park ❷** with its flower gardens and bandstand adds to the village-like atmosphere. There are often free concerts here on weekends. The park stretches for several blocks, with the railroad tracks running along the western side.

Above from far left:
Glasswork from the Charles Hosmer Morse Museum of American Art – First Presbyterian church window; wisteria library lamp; jeweled box showing the four seasons; window with peacock and peonies.

Sidewalk Arts Festival
Each year in March, the city hosts the Winter Park Sidewalk Arts Festival. The three-day event is one of the most prestigious outdoor arts festivals in the country. More than 225 artists from around the world and 350,000–400,000 visitors attend. For more information visit www.wpsaf.org.

Food and Drink 🍴

① THE BRIARPATCH RESTAURANT
252 N. Park Avenue; tel: 407-628-8651; $
A pretty spot for coffee or ice cream, as well as full meals. Watch the passing scene from the sidewalk tables. Open daily for breakfast, lunch, dinner.

② BOSPHORUS
108 S. Park Avenue, tel: 407-644-8609; $$
Serving Turkish cuisine, this popular restaurant is open for both lunch and dinner.

SCENIC BOAT TOUR

Turn left down Morse Boulevard and follow it to its end at Lake Osceola. Here, the **Scenic Boat Tour ❸** (312 E. Morse Blvd; tel: 407-644-4056; www.scenicboattours.com; daily 10am–4pm; charge) shows you Winter Park from a different perspective, with guides giving an entertaining commentary along the way. The one-hour cruise sails along three of the area's chain of lakes and through the historic canals that link them; these were dug in the late 1800s for logging operations and today are solely used for pleasure boats.

After passing several gorgeous homes – many of these large mansions were mere summer retreats for wealthy families – you pass the **Albin Polasek Museum & Sculpture Gardens ❹** (633 Osceola Avenue; tel: 407-647-6294; www.polasek.org; Tue–Sat

10am–4pm, Sun 1–4pm; charge). The Czech-American sculptor retired to this estate, and you can glimpse some of his works in the gardens. The museum contains many more of his paintings, drawings, and sculptures in addition to antiquities from his private collection.

The cruise then heads into the lush and overgrown Fern Canal which leads into Lake Virginia. From here you can see some of the landmarks of Rollins College, looking very pretty and peaceful from the water.

HANNIBAL SQUARE

After the cruise, return to Park Avenue. Turn left and carry on to the end of Central Park, then turn right on New England Avenue. Across the tracks, opposite the park's southwest corner, is the site of the Saturday

Below: Albin Polasek's beautiful sculpture gardens.

farmers' market. The small brick building alongside houses the **Winter Park Historical Museum ❺** (200 W. New England Avenue; tel: 407-647-8180; Thur–Fri 11am–3pm, Sat 9am–1pm, Sun 1–4pm; donation) with photographs, artifacts, and other exhibits on the community.

More boutique stores and restaurants line the next two blocks to **Hannibal Square ❻**. This was the heart of the black community, who moved here in the 1880s to work in railroad and domestic service jobs in the growing Winter Park community. A mural depicts an historic moment in 1887 when citizens crossed the railroad tracks to cast their votes and elected two African-American aldermen to Winter Park's town council.

In the next block, the **Hannibal Square Heritage Center ❼** (642 W. New England Avenue; tel: 407-539-2680; www.crealde.org; Tue–Sat) has exhibits, photographs, and oral histories gathered from members of the community, and hosts traveling exhibitions.

ROLLINS COLLEGE

Return to Park Avenue and continue south. A detour right along Lyman Avenue leads you to the **Winter Park Welcome Center and Chamber of Commerce** (151 W. Lyman Avenue; tel: 407-644-8281; www.winterpark.org), where you can pick up some maps and information.

Park Avenue ends at the grounds of Rollins College. Founded in 1885, it is Florida's oldest college. The attractive campus, with its original Spanish-Mediterranean-style buildings, spreads along the shores of Lake Virginia. Notice the Walk of Fame near the entrance, made of stepping stones gathered from places linked to famous historical figures.

Turn left on Holt Avenue and follow it to its end on the shores of the lake, where you can visit another of Winter Park's leading cultural attractions. **Cornell Fine Arts Museum ❽** (1000 Holt Avenue; tel: 407-646-2526; www.rollins.edu/cfam; Tue–Sat 10am–5pm, Sun 1–5pm; charge) has an excellent collection of European and American paintings, sculpture, and decorative art from the Renaissance to contemporary times, with changing exhibitions and artists' talks.

Also on campus are the Annie Russell Theatre and the Knowles Memorial Chapel, connected by a loggia. Both buildings were built in 1931–2 and feature on the US National Register of Historic Places.

Above from far left: the shops down Park Avenue; *Moonlight Seascape* (detail) by Thomas Moran (1837-1926), Cornell Fine Arts Museum.

Food and Drink 🍴

③ **BARNIE'S COFFEE AND TEA COMPANY**
118 S. Park Avenue; tel: 407-629-0042; $
The Barnie's chain is a local alternative to Starbucks where you'll find delicious coffee and sweet treats.

④ **EOLA WINE COMPANY**
136 S. Park Avenue; tel: 407-599-3399; $
There are tables inside and out where you can try some interesting wines, and have a light snack.

Parking
Winter Park is a popular place for Orlando residents too, especially on the weekends when they come for the farmers' market or to enjoy the scene along Park Avenue. Street parking can be tough to find, but there is free all-day parking in lots and garages on Canton Avenue by the railroad tracks, and across the tracks on either side of Morse Boulevard at New York Avenue.

NORTH OF ORLANDO

Just a few miles north of downtown Orlando, hotels and tourist attractions give way to the real world of central Florida. You'll find small, sleepy towns, natural springs, and state parks that harbor a wealth of wildlife, from fearsome alligators to gentle, endangered manatees.

> **DISTANCE** 40 miles (64km) to Blue Springs State Park from downtown Orlando
> **TIME** One day
> **START** Eatonville
> **END** Blue Springs State Park
> **POINTS TO NOTE**
> Stop off at Maitland on your way, or combine your trip with a visit to nearby Winter Park.

Florida's Birds
One of the functions of the Audubon Center for Birds of Prey is environmental education, so it's a good place not only to learn about these magnificent birds but also about Florida's habitat and natural resources.

A good way to balance the surreal world of the theme parks is to visit the real world of the natural parks, where you can enjoy the great outdoors and see some of central Florida's natural springs and amazing wildlife. This tour provides some suggestions that are right on Orlando's doorstep.

EATONVILLE

Take I-4 north to Lee Road, exit 88. Turn right (east) on Lee Road and then immediately left (north) on Wymore Road which runs parallel to the highway. Turn right on E. Kennedy Boulevard.

Eatonville is the oldest African-American township in the country, founded in 1883. Although most of

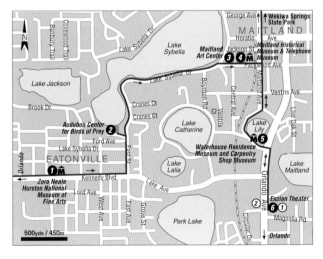

its original buildings are now gone, you can visit the **Zora Neale Hurston National Museum of Fine Arts ❶** (227 E. Kennedy Blvd; tel: 407-647-3307; www.zoranealehurston festival.com; Mon–Fri 9am–4pm; donation), dedicated to the town's most famous daughter. An author and folklorist, Hurston wrote about her early life in Eatonville in her novels *Their Eyes Were Watching God* and *Dust Tracks on a Road.*

AUDUBON CENTER FOR BIRDS OF PREY

Drive east along Kennedy Boulevard to East Street. Turn left on East Street, and after three blocks turn left on Audubon Way. This leads to the **Audubon Center for Birds of Prey ❷** (1101 Audubon Way; tel: 407-644-0190; www.audubonofflorida. org; Tue–Sun 10am–4pm; charge).

A non-profit raptor rehabilitation center, it rescues and cares for more than 600 injured, sick, and orphaned birds of prey each year. Over 40 percent of them are returned to the wild *(see also margin, left).*

MAITLAND

Return to East Street, turn left and follow the road around the shores of Lake Sybelia. Turn right on Packwood Avenue. Midway down this short street is the **Maitland Art Center ❸** (231 W. Packwood Avenue; tel: 407-539-2181; www. maitlandartcenter.org; Mon–Fri

9am–4.30pm, Sat–Sun noon–4.30pm; charge).

The center was founded as an art colony in the 1930s–1950s by artist and architect André Smith. Small cottages and studios are set around pretty grounds inside a walled garden, with murals, sculptures, and bas reliefs inspired by Aztec/Mayan designs. It offers galleries, workshops, concerts, and events.

Maitland Historical Museum and Telephone Museum
Next door is the **Maitland Historical Museum and Telephone Museum ❹** (221 W. Packwood Avenue; tel: 407-644-1364; www. maitlandhistory.org; Wed–Sun noon–4pm; charge). The former

Above from far left: the Maitland Art Center garden is dotted with lovely flowers and Aztec/ Mayan designs; Lake Lily wildlife.

The Florida Manatee

A subspecies of the West Indian manatee, the Florida manatee is native to Florida, the only place in the US where they live year-round. At home in both fresh and salt water, they are found in rivers, springs, harbors, inlets, and bays. Adults usually measure 9–10 feet (2.5–3 meters) long.

Although they spend most of their time underwater, manatees are mammals and must surface to breath. When resting they can stay submerged for up to 20 minutes. Early settlers hunted manatees for food and oil, and they are now an endangered species. Today boats are their greatest threat; the white markings you often see on a manatee's skin are scars from propeller injuries.

Alligators live in most of Florida's waterways, typ
eating fish, turtles, and other small animals.
alligators, however, occasionally attack larger an
such as deer, and may even attack humans.

St Johns River
At 310 miles
(500km) long, the
St Johns River is the
longest in Florida.
It is one of the few
major rivers that
flow north, and also
one of only 14 to be
designated an Ameri-
can Heritage River.

has exhibits on the early days of the
town and regional history, set in a
quaint house. Behind it, the Telephone Museum has a collection of
early phones and memorabilia.

*Waterhouse Residence Museum
and Carpentry Shop Museum*
Turn right on Maitland Avenue and
follow it for two blocks to the shores
of Lake Lily, a small, pretty lake
teeming with birdlife. You'll see
heron, egrets, muscovy ducks, turtles,
and possibly even alligators along the
shore. Follow the path around the
lake to visit the **Waterhouse Residence Museum and Carpentry
Shop Museum** ❺ (840 Lake Lily
Drive; tel: 407-644-2451; Wed–Sun
noon–4pm; charge), which give a
glimpse of the lifestyle of a middle-
class pioneer family in the 1880s.

Enzian Theater
If you're visiting Maitland at the end
of the day and fancy an unusual
evening out, turn right out of the
parking area onto Orlando Avenue
and drive a few blocks south to
Magnolia Road where you'll find
the **Enzian Theater** ❻, see ⓡ①
(1300 S. Orlando Avenue; tel: 407-
629-0054; www.enzian.org; hours
and admission vary). At this alternative cinema you can have a drink
and a meal while watching first-run
independent features.

Also nearby is **Buca di Beppo**, see
ⓡ②, a fun Italian restaurant.

WEKIWA SPRINGS STATE PARK

To continue north, take Maitland
Avenue north to Maitland Boulevard and turn left, which leads back
to I-4. After 7¹⁄₂ miles (12km), take
exit 94. Turn left (west) on Route
434 and then right on Wekiwa
Springs Road. This brings you to the
entrance to **Wekiwa Springs State
Park** ❼ (1800 Wekiwa Circle,
Apoka; tel: 407-884-2008; www.
floridastateparks.org/wekiwasprings;
daily 8am–sunset; charge).

With enormous oak and cypress
trees, this beautiful 7,800-acre
(3,160-hectare) park, just 20 minutes north of the city, is a favorite
get-away for Orlando residents. You
can swim in a natural spring, or rent
canoes to paddle along the Wekiwa
River and Rock Springs Run. There
are also hiking and biking trails.

Food and Drink

① ENZIAN THEATER
1300 S. Orlando Avenue; tel: 407-629-0054; $
Choose from a tasty menu of sandwiches, pizza, pasta, salads,
shared plates and desserts, and there is a selection of wines
and beers as well as coffees and organic teas.

② BUCA DI BEPPO
1351 S. Orlando Avenue; tel: 407-622-7663; open for dinner
and Sun lunch; $$
The walls are covered with cheerful art and photos, the tables are
covered with huge plates of great Italian food meant to be shared.

**③ LAZY GATOR BAR AND BLACK HAMMOCK
RESTAURANT**
2356 Black Hammock Fish Camp Road, Oviedo; lunch and
dinner; tel: 407-977-8235; $–$$
The full-menu restaurant serves gator bites, catfish, and Florida
seafood favorites. Two lakeside bars have live entertainment
Friday and Saturday nights and Sunday afternoons.

LAKE JESSUP

Alternatively, to travel the central Florida waters at a faster pace, turn right on Route 434 from the interstate and head east to Lake Jessup. Turn left on DeLeon Street, then left on Howard Avenue. This curves towards the lake and becomes Black Hammock Road, then Black Hammock Fish Camp Road. Park at the marina.

A 30-minute airboat ride with **Black Hammock Airboat Adventure ❽** (2356 Black Hammock Fish Camp Road, Oviedo; tel: 407-977-8235; www.blackhammockairboat rides.com; 9.30am–5.30pm; charge) is a great way to explore this lake on the edge of what is often called the Central Florida Everglades. The lake is home to bald eagles, a host of birdlife, bobcats, turtles and more than 10,000 alligators. If you don't spot one, you can see them in the live gator exhibit. Afterwards enjoy the views from the **Lazy Gator Bar and Black Hammock Restaurant**, see ⓦ③.

BLUE SPRINGS STATE PARK

In the winter, a rare chance to see manatees in the wild awaits further north at **Blue Springs State Park ❾** (2100 W. French Avenue, Orange City; tel: 386-775-3663; www.florida stateparks.org/bluespring; daily 8am–sunset; charge). From I-4, take exit 104 and follow US 17/92 to Orange City. Turn west on French Avenue and follow it until the pavement ends; turn left for the park entrance.

Set along the St Johns River, this beautiful park contains large natural springs which are a winter refuge for the manatee. The manatees swim upriver from November to March to shelter in the warm waters *(see margin, right)*.

During the summer when the manatees have gone, you can swim, snorkel and tube in the springs. You can also rent canoes and kayaks, and there are picnic areas, campsites, and hiking trails. The **Louis Thursby House**, former home of a pioneer citrus grower, is open Wednesday to Sunday. Thursby's Blue Spring Landing, once a busy port for paddle wheelers, is now the departure point for St Johns River Cruises (tel: 386-917-0724; www.sjriver cruises.com), which offer two-hour nature cruises through this remarkable ecosystem.

Above from far left: kayaks for hire; no swimming!; birdlife in the Blue Spring State Park.

Manatee Refuge February is the top viewing month to see manatees at the Blue Springs State Park. A boardwalk with viewing platforms runs along the springs, and on a good day you can see dozens of these giant, gentle creatures submerged just below the clear surface. They look like grey shadows at first, until you see them roll or stick the tip of their nose up for air.

14

THE SPACE COAST

Many visitors make a daytrip to the Kennedy Space Center, under an hour's drive from Orlando. But with a superb wildlife refuge, pristine national seashore and the attractions of Cocoa Beach, the Space Coast is well worth further exploration.

DISTANCE 180 miles (290km)

TIME One to two days

START Orlando

END Cocoa Village

POINTS TO NOTE

A stay in the surf capital of Cocoa Beach for a night or two is recommended to take in the area's other highlights. *For hotels, see p.117.*

Nature and Space
Only about 10% of the Kennedy Space Center's 140,000 acres (34,000 hectares) is used for the space program. The rest is a designated nature reserve. On the KSC bus tour, keep an eye out for alligators sunning beside the ponds. You may also see some of the reserve's 10,000 wild pigs. Drivers will point out enormous eagle's nests; there are now 16 nests in the reserve, some measuring 7ft (2 meters) wide and weighing around 1,000 pounds (450kg).

The Atlantic beaches of Florida's Space Coast are the closest beaches to Orlando. Spread along barrier islands, they are connected to the mainland by causeways across the broad Indian and Banana rivers.

KENNEDY SPACE CENTER

Leave Orlando on Toll Road 528, known as the Beachline Expressway (or Beeline Expressway, depending on which map you're looking at). Turn left (north) on SR 407 and right (east) on SR405, which leads to the **Kennedy Space Center Visitor Complex ①** (State Road 405, Merritt Island; tel: 321-449-4444; www.kennedyspace center.com; daily from 9am; charge).

Although at first glance it appears small compared to the theme parks,

even with a full day you'll be hard pressed to fit everything in. In addition to the visitor complex, a main component is the Space Center bus tour which takes you to three outlying sites. This alone takes around three hours, as much time is spent getting on and off the buses and lining up for the next leg of the tour. A daily schedule which gives starting times for the various films and attractions is included with your map of the complex.

If you run out of time to see everything, you can validate your ticket at the exit for a second day's admission within seven days of your first visit.

The Visitor Complex

Walk through the information center to the outdoor plaza. To the left is Astronaut Encounter, where you can meet an astronaut who has flown into space.

Food and Drink 🍴

① **LUNCH WITH AN ASTRONAUT**
Kennedy Space Center Visitor Complex; tel: 321-449-4400; $$
After a buffet lunch, an astronaut presents an entertaining and informative talk on his or her experiences in space, answers questions, and signs autographs. Book ahead as places are limited.

Through the archway is the Rocket Garden with an impressive array of historic rockets from early space missions. Try and catch one of the enlightening 15-minute guided tours. Here you can have **Lunch with an Astronaut**, see ⑪①.

Some attractions are geared for younger visitors, such as Robot Scouts and Mad Mission to Mars: 2025. Behind the latter is a building containing the IMAX theaters. The best of the two films is *Space Station 3D*, narrated by Tom Cruise. The footage was shot by astronauts during actual missions, and gives you a real sense of what it's like to live and work at the International Space Station. *Magnificent Desolation: Walking on the Moon 3D*, produced by Tom Hanks, follows the Apollo astronauts' lunar footsteps.

In the far right corner of the complex, the Shuttle Launch Experience recreates the sensations of blasting off into space, minus the centrifugal force that causes motion sickness. Opposite, you can walk through a replica Shuttle Explorer.

Space Center Tours

Nearby is the departure point for the KSC bus tour, which runs every 15 minutes. The drivers give a running commentary, and point out the resident wildlife *(see margin, left)*.

The first leg of the tour takes you past the enormous Vehicle Assembly Building, where the rockets are put together. At 525-feet (160-meters) tall it is the largest single-story building in the world. The bus stops at the LC-39 Observation Gantry, where you can see the launch pads in the distance.

The second stop of the tour, at the Apollo/Saturn V Center, is the most exciting. Here you can walk around and under a fully restored Saturn V moon rocket, and watch a fascinating

Above from far left: astronauts preparing for launch; the Rocket Garden; another successful landing for the shuttle Endeavour.

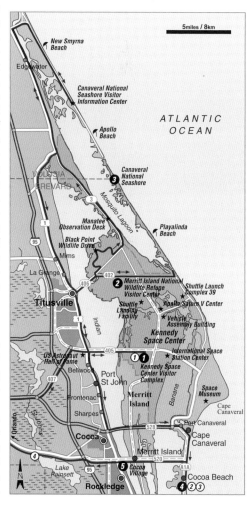

multimedia recreation of the first Saturn V manned mission launch.

The third stop, at the International Space Station Center, is a bit of an anticlimax, with a walk-through past models of parts of the space station.

US Astronaut Hall of Fame

Your ticket also includes admission to the US Astronaut Hall of Fame, in a separate building back across the causeway from the visitor complex. In addition to exhibits honoring the astronauts, it contains simulators that let you try out a variety of space experiences, from riding a moon rover to space walking in lunar gravity to landing a space shuttle.

MERRITT ISLAND WILDLIFE

There is no public access beyond the space center visitor complex, so you must drive back across the SR 405

Shuttle Schedule
The Merritt Island National Wildlife Refuge is closed three days in advance of space shuttle launches, so check the shuttle schedule when planning your trip. If you want to view a launch, packages are available from Kennedy Space Center – check the website for further details (www.kennedy spacecenter.com). Alternatively, you can view the launch from along US Highway 1 North, near Titusville, where you can see the launch pad across the Indian River.

causeway and north on US 1 through Titusville to reach the **Merritt Island National Wildlife Refuge ❷** (tel: 321-861-0667; www.fws.gov/merritt island; open sunrise–sunset). It is sign-posted from town – take SR 406/402 (Garden Street). If you are coming from I-95 take exit 220.

Start at the **Visitor Center** (Mon–Fri 8am–4.30pm, Sat–Sun 9am–5pm), where you can pick up maps and information about the wildlife, walking trails and drives in the reserve. Some 43 miles (69km) long, the island is the habitat for over 500 wildlife species, many of which are threatened or endangered. In addition to osprey, bald eagles, heron, egrets and pelicans, you may see alligators, raccoons, wild hogs and river otters.

Highly recommended is the Black Point Wildlife Drive, a 7-mile (11-km) self-guided tour through one of the best wildlife viewing areas, with information on 12 numbered stops. Just before stop 11, watch for the large alligator often seen sunning him-(her?)self on the right side of the road.

Another highlight is the Manatee Observation Deck beside the Haulover Canal on SR 3. Manatees *(see box, p.83)* thrive here year-round, thanks to a ban on motorized vessels in the surrounding area, and are most frequently seen in spring and autumn.

CANAVERAL NATIONAL SEASHORE

Adjacent to the wildlife refuge is the **Canaveral National Seashore ❸** (tel: 321-267-1110; charge). At the

southern end, lovely Playalinda Beach is accessible via SR 402 through the reserve. To reach Apollo Beach at the northern end, drive north on SR 3 and US 1 to SR A1A, where you'll also find the visitor center, walking trails and other facilities. In between are miles of beautiful, undeveloped stretches of beach backed by barrier dunes and the Mosquito Lagoon. This area provides a haven for loggerhead turtles, fish and shellfish, waterfowl, migrating birds and, of course, human beachcombers.

COCOA BEACH

Take US Highway 1 south and turn left (east) on SR 528. After passing Cape Canaveral and Port Canaveral, with its busy cruise terminal, the road curves south towards **Cocoa Beach ❹**. Known as Florida's surf capital, it has long stretches of broad sandy beach, a laid-back, youthful vibe, and a string of good restaurants and bars.

The town's landmark is the Cocoa Beach Pier, which juts 800 feet (245 meters) out above the ocean from Meade Avenue. The arcade atop its rustic wooden pylons is lined with restaurants, bars, shops and a fishing deck. **Mai Tiki Bar**, see ⑪②, is a great spot to view the sunset.

On the corner of SR 520 and Atlantic Avenue you'll find the 'one of a kind' Ron Jon Surf Shop, a temple to the glorified beach lifestyle filled with surf clothes, accessories and boards of every size and style, and open 24 hours. Next door is the Cocoa

Beach Surf Company Surf Complex, selling more beach gear and with its own shark-filled aquarium. The **Shark Pit** nearby, see ⑪③, is a relaxing bar and restaurant.

Take SR 520 across three causeways to the west side of the Indian River. Turn left on Brevard Avenue to reach **Cocoa Village ❺**, an artsy enclave of historic buildings that now house galleries, antiques shops, boutiques, and specialty stores.

Continue west on SR 520. Four miles (6km) past the junction of I-95, before you cross the St Johns River, look out on your left for the **Lone Cabbage Fish Camp**, see ⑪④. This rustic roadhouse-style bar and restaurant is a popular place for airboat rides along the river, spotting alligators and other wildlife.

Beyond the bridge, SR 520 curves north to intersect with SR 528 which will take you back to Orlando.

Above from far left: birds line up; Cocoa Beach pier.

Above: don't be fooled by the smile; colorful butterfly.

Food and Drink ⑪

② MAI TIKI BAR
Cocoa Beach Pier; tel: 321-783-7549; $
Enjoy a drink and panoramic ocean views from the end of the Cocoa Beach Pier. The pier also has four restaurants and an ice cream parlor.

③ SHARK PIT
4001 N. Atlantic Avenue in the Cocoa Beach Surf Company complex; tel: 321-868-8952; $–$$.
Great spot for a casual drink or meal, with brick-oven pizzas, salads, sandwiches, and tropical-inspired entrées.

④ LONE CABBAGE FISH CAMP
SR 520 at St Johns River; tel: 321-632-4199; $
Try alligator tail, turtle, catfish, and other local favorites at this rustic riverside bar and restaurant. Lunch and dinner. Live music on Sunday afternoons.

TAMPA BAY

Another great theme park, Busch Gardens Africa, draws many visitors to Tampa Bay. But with beautiful Gulf Coast beaches, a scenic river, good art museums, the Florida Aquarium and an historic district to explore, there are plenty of reasons to extend your stay.

DISTANCE 120 miles (190km)

TIME One to three days

START Orlando

END Fort De Soto Park

POINTS TO NOTE

Traffic can be heavy in the metro area, especially on I-275 across Tampa Bay, so allow extra time to arrive at your destination.

Busch Gardens Shuttle

If you just want to visit Busch Gardens Africa and don't want to drive, consider taking the Busch Gardens Shuttle Express, which provides round-trip transportation from several Orlando locations ($10 per person at press time). For more information tel: 1-800-221-1339.

With its busy port and downtown business district, the city of Tampa is the commercial center of Florida's Gulf coast. Across Tampa Bay lies St Petersburg and Clearwater, the largest of the communities covering the Pinellas Peninsula, with a string of barrier-island beaches along the Gulf of Mexico. Together they form one of Florida's largest metropolitan areas with a population rivaling Miami's, but on the whole the bay area maintains a relaxed, casual atmosphere.

Tampa is only an hour's drive (or less) from Orlando, and even if you only have a day to spare, an excursion here gives you plenty of variety and a chance to see this vibrant Gulf coast region. This tour takes in some of the highlights of Tampa Bay, from Tampa's northeast corner, downtown to Ybor

City, across the bay to St Petersburg and on to Fort De Soto Park, with one of the country's most beautiful beaches.

CANOE ESCAPE

The Hillsborough River runs 54 miles (87km) from Green Swamp to Tampa Bay. Fed by pure water from Crystal Springs, it provides around 75 percent of the city's drinking water. Some 20 miles (32km) of the river are protected in a wilderness park, providing a rich habitat for migrating birds and local wildlife. It's one of the best wildlife viewing spots in all of Florida. The ideal way to see it is from the river itself, on a canoe or kayak trip with **Canoe Escape ❶** (9335 East Fowler Avenue, Thonotosassa, FL 33592; tel: 813-986-2067; www.canoeescape.com; Mon–Fri 9am–5pm, Sat–Sun 8am–5pm; charge).

From Orlando, take I-4 West to I-75 (exit 9). Go north on I-75 to Fowler Avenue (exit 265). Exit to your right (east). Canoe Escape is located half a mile (800 meters) on your right on Fowler Avenue, directly across from the Big Top Flea Market.

Most trips are self-guided and range from 4¹⁄₂ miles (14km; 2 hours) to 9 miles (7km; 4 hours). There is a longer trip for seasoned paddlers. Transporta-

tion and orientation is provided. Interpretive guided trips with an experienced guide are also available.

This peaceful and scenic river, lined with cypress, oaks, and thick woodlands, truly is an escape from the busy cities and theme parks. Paddling here is gentle and relaxed, yet there's a real sense of adventure as you glide along the banks, looking for wildlife. Two of the top birds to see are limpkins and Roseatte spoonbills, both prominent in Central and South America and at the top of their range here in Florida. Depending on conditions and the season, you may see alligators, turtles, wild pigs, raccoons, and a variety of herons, egrets, hawks, woodpeckers, kingfishers, wood storks, and anhingas.

BUSCH GARDENS AFRICA

Wildlife of a larger variety can be seen two miles (3km) west of I-75 (exit 54)

Above from far left:
a canoe trip along the river allows you to get close to all the wildlife.

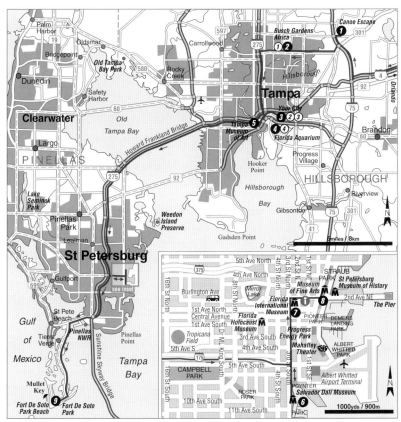

A Little Hospitality
At Busch Gardens, be sure to visit the Hospitality House in the Bird Gardens area where you can have a free sample of Anheuser-Busch beers. Or sign up for one of the BrewMasters Club tastings, which take place throughout the day. You can try some of the latest brews and learn about beer and food pairings. It's fun and informative, and you'll get to try some new beers before they hit the general market.

at **Busch Gardens Africa ➋** (3605 E. Bougainvillea Avenue, Tampa; tel: 813-987-5280 or 888-800-5447; www.buschgardens.com; daily 10am–6pm, extended hours summer and vacations; charge). This popular theme park, owned and operated by the Anheuser-Busch brewery, combines spectacular thrill rides with one of the country's largest zoos.

More than 2,000 exotic animals, including several endangered species, live in natural habitats resembling those of their native Africa. The largest is the 65-acre (26-hectare) Serengeti Plain, where zebras, giraffe, black rhino, impalas, waterbuck, and other beasts roam freely. You can view them

from a train that goes around the plain or from the Skyride that goes over it.

For a closer encounter, take the Serengeti Safari (extra charge), a half-hour, off-road ride in a flatbed truck across the middle of the reserve. You'll stop and hand-feed the giraffe along the way.

Walk along the Edge of Africa for a look at lions and hyenas (isolated from the Serengeti Plain for obvious reasons) and hippos swimming in their pool. Another highlight is the Myombe Reserve, where you can see gorillas and chimpanzees in a rain-forest environment.

Orangutans and a Bengal tiger are among the exotic animals in Jungala, the park's newest attraction, which opened in the Congo area in spring 2008. This colorful village features amazing trees, waterfalls, caves, and underwater windows that let you connect to the animals' jungle world.

Near the entrance to the park in Morocco, **Sultan's Sweets**, see ⑪①, is a good spot for breakfast or for coffee and refreshments at any time of the day.

Busch Gardens contains some of the region's most awesome thrill rides. SheiKra is a terrifying dive coaster that takes you 200ft (60 meters) up, then 90 degrees straight down in a floorless car going 70mph (110 kmh). More death-defying loops, dives, drops, and inversions are in store on the Kumba and Montu roller coasters at opposite ends of the park. Gwazi is the largest, fastest, double wooden roller coaster in the southeast. White-water rapids, flume rides, and tamer

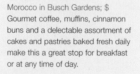

Food and Drink 🍴

① SULTAN'S SWEETS
Morocco in Busch Gardens; $
Gourmet coffee, muffins, cinnamon buns and a delectable assortment of cakes and pastries baked fresh daily make this a great stop for breakfast or at any time of day.

② CENTRO YBOR
8th Avenue between 15th and 17th streets; www.centroybor.com; $
Covering two-blocks, this complex has several good bars, including the Tampa Bay Brewing Co. and Adobe Gilas, as well as cafés and restaurants for a coffee or quick bite to eat.

③ LA TROPICANA CAFÉ
1822 E. 7th Avenue; tel: 813-247-4040; Mon–Sat 7am–3pm; $
Have a traditional Ybor City breakfast of Cuban toast and café con leche, old-fashioned Cuban sandwiches, Spanish bean soup and other local favorites.

rides for younger visitors are also spread throughout the park.

YBOR CITY

Take Busch Boulevard west to I-275, and take it south to downtown Tampa and **Ybor City ❸**, one of the bay area's most historic districts. This is Tampa's Latin Quarter, founded in 1886 when Vicente Martinez Ybor moved his cigar-manufacturing business here from Key West. Master cigar craftsmen and workers from Cuba, Spain and Italy came and made their homes in this vibrant multicultural neighborhood. At one time there were 200 cigar factories in Ybor City, with hundreds of workers in each one.

The red-brick buildings, wrought-iron balconies and brick-lined streets survive, making it one of the most charming areas of the city. The cigar shops, still prominent here, have been joined by trendy shops and vintage clothing boutiques. After dark, Ybor City is Tampa's liveliest nightlife area.

The heart of the district along 7th Avenue – La Setima – is lined with bars, clubs, restaurants, cafés, and cigar bars, which come into their own after 5pm. **Centro Ybor**, see ⑪②, has several good bars and cafés. **La Tropicana Café**, see ⑪③, is a traditional spot for breakfast and lunch. Further along 7th Avenue is the beautiful tiled facade of the Columbia Restaurant *(see p.121)*, a local institution.

A Saturday market takes place in Centennial Park at 9th Avenue and 19th Street. Opposite is the Ybor City Museum State Park (1818 9th Avenue; tel: 813-247-6323; www.floridastateparks.org; daily 9am–5pm; charge), set in an old bakery dating from 1896. Here you can watch some of the last of the master cigar rollers at work, and take a walking tour of the district. Next door, several small cottages, or casitas, where the workers once lived provide a truly fascinating look at the life of the community.

Above from far left: poster showing the old cigar rollers at work, Ybor City Museum State Park; cigar signs are ubiquitous in Ybor City; monument to the immigrants; La Setima neon lights.

Water and Wildlife

The Hillsborough River compares with the Everglades as a top spot to view Florida wildlife. Because it is spring-fed, it doesn't depend on rainwater to keep it flowing. Canoe and kayak trips continue even during the dry season. In fact, the best time to come is when the water levels are low because the wildlife has to come to the river to drink when the ponds and springs dry up inland. The logs are exposed and you can see alligators and turtles out sunning.

Each season is unique, with different wildlife to see. Varying water levels make a big difference to the appearance of the river. The wildlife season starts in October as the gators start to come out. In November–December migratory birds show up. The peak wildlife viewing time is March–May, when it's not uncommon to be paddling 10 feet (3 meters) from an alligator or a bunch of baby alligators. The water level is at its lowest in May and at its highest in September, with a variable of around 6 feet (2 meters).

Above from left to right: a dolphin smile; a lionfish at the Florida Aquarium; stripes galore; ferries to get around.

Above: do not feed the dolphins!

Below: impressive artwork at the Arts Center Gallery in St Petersburg.

FLORIDA AQUARIUM

From Ybor City, take 13th Street south toward the port, where it becomes Channelside Drive. Follow signs for the **Florida Aquarium ❹** (701 Channelside Drive; tel: 813-273-4000; www.flaquarium.org; daily 9.30am–5pm; charge), home to more than 20,000 aquatic plants and marine animals from around the world.

Starting on the upper level, the route follows a drop of rain on its journey to the depths of the ocean, passing through a variety of watery habitats starting with Florida's wetlands, where you'll see playful river otters and free-flying birds. Highlights include the colorful tropical fish in the coral reefs, and the fascinating leafy sea dragons, which look like seahorses dressed up for Mardi Gras. All kinds of predators, from sharks to lionfish to moray eels, are displayed in the Sea Hunt exhibit.

This excellent aquarium has numerous shows and demonstrations throughout the day which both educate and entertain. Among the favorites are the Penguin Promenade and Otterology. There's also an outdoor play area for children with water jets and a pirate ship.

For refreshments, head for the nearby **Channelside**, see ⑪④, complex, where you'll find a wealth of bars and restaurants.

TAMPA MUSEUM OF ART

Continue along the channel and turn right (north) on Franklin Street to reach downtown Tampa. On the banks of the Hillsborough River is the **Tampa Museum of Art ❺** (600 N. Ashley Drive; tel: 813-274-8130; www.tampamuseum.com; Tue–Sat 10am–5pm, Sun 11am–5pm; charge). It contains a fine collection of Greek and Roman antiquities, as well as artworks from the 20th century to the present. There is a sculpture garden along the river.

SALVADOR DALÍ MUSEUM

The area's most impressive museum lies across Tampa Bay in St Petersburg. Take I-275 south across the Howard Frankland Bridge. Then take I-175 East (exit 22, on your left) towards Tropicana Field. Follow it to the end, then continue through the light and turn right on 3rd Street South. After about half a mile (800 meters) you'll reach the **Salvador Dalí Museum ❻** (1000 Third Street

South, St Petersburg; tel: 727-823-3767; www.salvadordalimuseum.org; Mon–Sat 9.30am–5.30pm, Thur until 8pm, Fri until 6.30pm, Sun noon–5.30pm; charge).

This excellent museum, one of the best in the South, houses the largest collection of Dalí's works outside of Spain. Among its 2,140 pieces are six master works measuring over 5ft (1.5 meters). It is based on the private collection amassed by A. Reynolds Morse, a Cleveland industrialist, and his wife Eleanor.

The works are displayed on a rotating basis, in changing exhibitions that also incorporate works on loan from top collections around the world. Take a free tour for a fascinating insight into the artist and his works.

FLORIDA INTERNATIONAL MUSEUM AND MUSEUM OF FINE ARTS

Two more art museums are nearby in downtown St Petersburg. Drive north on 3rd Street South and turn right on 2nd Avenue North to reach the **Florida International Museum ❼** (244 Second Avenue North; tel: 727-341-7900; www.floridamuseum.org; Tue–Sat 9/10am–5/6pm, Sun noon–5pm; charge). It stages world-class temporary exhibitions on diverse subjects from medieval art to American Art Nouveau.

Continue on 2nd Avenue North to the waterfront and the **Museum of Fine Arts ❽** (255 Beach Drive N.E.; tel: 727-896-2667; www.fine-arts.org; Tue–Sat 10am–5pm, Sun 1–5pm;

charge). Monet, Renoir, Cézanne, Gauguin, Rodin and O'Keeffe are among the major artists represented here. There is an outstanding photography collection, Steuben glass, and collections of pre-Columbian, Native American, African, and Asian art.

FORT DE SOTO PARK AND BEACH

You're spoiled for choice with the string of beaches ranging all the way along the barrier islands on the Gulf Coast. For a real gem, however, take I-275 south to the Pinellas Bayway (toll) to reach **Fort De Soto Park ❾** (3500 Pinellas Bayway S.; Tierra Verde; tel: 727-582-2267; www.fortdesoto.com).

With good swimming and three miles (5km) of pure white sand, Fort DeSoto Park beach is regularly named as one of the best beaches in the US. The park contains an historic fort built during the Spanish-American War, fishing piers, campsites, and walking trails through a wild, natural landscape. Visit during the week and you may find you have it largely to yourself.

Tampa Bay Trolleys

Tampa Bay's first electric streetcar lines were built in 1892; by 1926 they had become an essential means of transport, with nearly 24 million passengers. But two decades later they were discontinued after World War II. Today, trolleys are rolling through the city once again. In Tampa, the In-Town Trolley purple line serves Downtown and Harbour Island while the green line makes a loop through Downtown and the Channel District. The TECO line streetcar connects Ybor City to these areas. Downtown St Petersburg is served by the Looper Trolley, while the Suncoast Beach Trolley makes its way along the Gulf Coast.

Food and Drink 🍴

④ **CHANNELSIDE**
Channelside Drive; tel: 813-223-4250; www.ChannelsideTampa.com; $–$$
Next door to the Florida Aquarium, this shopping, dining, and entertainment complex offers a variety of choices for refreshments, from Margarita Mama's and Tina Tapa's, to the southern cooking and music at Stump's Supper Club.

DIRECTORY

A user-friendly alphabetical listing of practical information, plus hand-picked hotels and restaurants, clearly organized by area, to suit all budgets and tastes.

A

AGE RESTRICTIONS

You have to be over 21 to drink alcohol; even if you are considerably older than that, you should carry photo identification with you. If you cannot prove your age, you will not be served.

Many of the rides in theme parks specify height restrictions. Check the relevant website for details.

B

BUSINESS HOURS

Outside the resorts, most businesses are open 9am–5pm, with many of the shopping malls opening at 10am and remaining open as late as 10pm. Many large supermarkets and numerous restaurants stay open 24 hours.

Banks usually remain open until at least 4pm from Monday through Thursday, and until 6pm on Friday. Some banks are open for a short time on Saturday.

During some public holidays, local banks, businesses, stores, and attractions may close.

C

CLIMATE

Central Florida has a subtropical climate, with high humidity. Summer daytime temperatures average 80°F–90°F (27°C–32°C) but can feel much hotter in July–August. Winter weather is dry and temperate, with daytime temperatures averaging 71°F–80°F (22°C–27°C), though they can drop surprisingly low at night.

Between May and September, heavy thunderstorms can occur almost every afternoon, but they are usually short in duration. Florida is unofficially dubbed the 'lightning capital of the country.' This is attributed to the hot, wet air that lies close to the ground, and unstable atmospheric conditions that exist during this period.

If you see dark clouds and flashes of lightning approaching, take cover. If in a car, stay inside until the storm passes. If in a building, don't 'make a run for it.' Many lightning victims are killed when getting into or out of their cars. Boaters should head for the nearest place they can tie up and evacuate the boat. During any nearby lightning storm, parks will close their outdoor attractions.

Florida ranks eighth in the list of US states with the most tornadoes per year, but they're not nearly as bad as the awesome twisters that assail the Midwest. Trailer parks are particularly vulnerable. June to November is hurricane season, although Orlando is more protected than coastal cities.

CRIME AND SAFETY

Although Orlando is not a high crime area, it pays to take the same precautions you'd take in any city. Watch your wallet or handbag in crowded places and never leave valuable items unattended. Keep money and jewelry in

your hotel safe. Keep hotel room and patio doors locked even when you're in the room. Don't open the door unless you know who is there; use the safety chain or check with the front desk if in doubt.

When driving, keep doors locked and only park in well-lit areas. Never leave valuables in your car.

Theme parks conduct bag searches for all visitors and generally have good security.

Never approach or try to feed wildlife, especially alligators. Watch where you step when walking near a lake shore or wetland area.

CUSTOMS REGULATIONS

There is no limit on the amount of money – US or foreign traveler's checks or money orders – that you may bring into or take out of the US. But you must declare amounts exceeding $10,000 or the foreign currency equivalent.

Customs Allowances

Alcohol: Visitors over the age of 21 are permitted to bring in 34fl oz (1 liter) of alcohol for their personal use. Excess quantities are subject to duty and tax.
Cigars and Cigarettes: Visitors may bring in not more than 200 cigarettes (one carton), 50 cigars (as long as they are not Cuban), or 3lbs (1.3kg) of tobacco, or proportionate amounts of each. An additional 100 cigars may be brought in under your gift exemption.
Gifts: As a visitor to the US, you can claim on entry up to $100 worth of merchandise, free of duty and tax, as

gifts for other people. Such articles may have to be inspected, so do not gift-wrap them until after you have entered the country.

Prohibited Goods

Articles which visitors are forbidden to take into the US include: liquor-filled chocolates or candy, dangerous drugs, obscene publications, hazardous articles (e.g. fireworks), and narcotics.

Travelers using medicines containing narcotics (such as tranquilizers or cough medicine) should carry a prescription and/or a note from their doctor, and should take only the quantity required for a short stay. The medicine must be in its original, clearly labelled container. The medication must also be able to be legally prescribed in the US.

Meat and poultry, fruit and vegetables, most dairy, absinthe, more than 9 ounces (250 grams) caviar, and Cuban cigars are all prohibited.

D

DISABLED TRAVELERS

Accessibility and facilities are excellent at the theme parks and other attractions in Orlando. Special parking is available near the entrances to each park, the hotels, and other facilities.

Wheelchairs are available for rent in limited numbers in several locations, usually near the park's entrance. For some attractions and rides, guests may remain in wheelchairs. For others, they must be able to leave the wheelchair.

Golf

There are 176 golf courses in the Orlando area, including many signature courses designed by famous golf pros. Orlando also hosts more professional golf tournaments than any other city. Visitor options range from public courses where you can play a casual round to all-inclusive golf resorts. For information on the range of golf resorts and facilities, contact the Official Visitor Center *(see p.105)*. The Golfer's Guide, a free publication (http://orlando. golfersguide.com) is also a good source of information.

Regulations are clearly indicated in leaflets and at the appropriate entrance. Some motorized wheelchairs are available for rent, and nearly all buses and launches can accommodate conventional wheelchairs. Wheelchair access is available at toilets in all the theme parks.

For hearing-impaired guests, there is a TDD at City Hall in Magic Kingdom, at Guest Services in Hollywood Studios, Epcot and Animal Kingdom, and at both Universal parks. Many rides and attractions have closed captioning. A sign-language interpreter is available for theater shows.

Sight-impaired guests can borrow complimentary cassettes and tape recorders at the same locations. A deposit is required.

E

ELECTRICITY

You'll need an adapter for most British and European plugs, as well as a voltage transformer. US sockets take flat two-pronged plugs and the power supply is 110–120 volts AC (60 cycles).

EMBASSIES AND CONSULATES

Most embassies are in Washington DC. These are the nearest consulates for English-speaking countries:
Australia: 2103 Coral Way, Suite 108, Miami, FL 33145; tel: 305-858-7633.
Canada: 200 South Biscayne Boulevard, Suite 1600, Miami, Florida 33131; tel: 305-579-1600.

New Zealand: 37 Observatory Circle, NW, Washington DC 20008; tel: 202-328-4800.
Republic of Ireland: 345 Park Avenue, 17th Floor, New York, NY 10022; tel: 212-319-2555.
South Africa: 333 East 38th Street, 9th Floor, New York, NY 10016; tel: 212-213-4880.
UK: 200 South Orange Avenue, Suite 2110, Orlando, FL 32801; tel: 407-426-7855.

EMERGENCY NUMBERS

For police, ambulance or fire services, dial: 911.

G

GAY AND LESBIAN TRAVELERS

For a few days every June, Orlando and its theme parks are host to Gay Days, when thousands of gays and lesbians come along to join in the special gay-oriented celebrations. For more details, log onto www.gaydays.com.

H

HEALTH

In the event you need medical assistance, ask the reception staff at your hotel. The larger resort hotels may well have a resident doctor, or the staff can help you find the nearest doctor or hospital.

MOSQUITO

Above from far left: Orlando is great for golfers; an Irish visitor shows his national colours; family fun on the beach; watch out for mosquitoes.

Insurance: The cost of even basic health care is exorbitant. Never leave home without adequate travel insurance; a minimum coverage of $1 million unlimited medical cover is strongly recommended.

There is nothing cheap about being sick in the US, whether it involves a simple visit to the doctor or a spell in a hospital. The initial emergency room fee charged by a good hospital might be $250 or more, and that's before the additional cost of X-rays, medicines, and so on have been added. It is therefore essential to have adequate medical insurance, and to carry an identification card or policy number at all times to ensure you receive prompt treatment.

Pharmacies: Always bring enough prescription medicines from home to cover the length of your trip. The cost of prescription medicine in the US is extremely high, and the same drugs may not be available.

For over-the-counter medicines, look for branches of Walgreens or CVS; many are open 24 hours. Wal-Mart, Target, and other retailers also have pharmacy sections.

Health Hazards: The two most common health hazards in Orlando are sunburn and heat exhaustion; both are easily avoided. Always use a high-factor sun cream and wear a hat and sunglasses.

The heat alone can be a danger, especially for the elderly or those with a pre-existing medical condition. Dehydration and salt deficiency can lead to heat exhaustion. The main symptoms are headache, weakness, lightheadedness, muscle aches, cramps, and agitation. Make a point of drinking plenty of non-alcoholic fluids (before you get thirsty), and take periodic breaks in the shade or in an air-conditioned environment.

If untreated, heat exhaustion can escalate to a far more serious case of heatstroke, which means that the body's temperature rises to dangerous levels. In addition to the symptoms listed above, people suffering from heatstroke may exhibit confusion, strange behavior, and even seizures. If you suspect a companion is suffering from heatstroke, get them to a cool place, apply cold damp cloths, and call for a doctor immediately.

I

INTERNET

There is free wireless internet access throughout Orlando International Airport. More and more hotels are offering complimentary high-speed internet access in their rooms and public areas. High-end hotels generally still charge (highly) for this service. Wireless access is often available in coffee shops such as Starbucks.

L

LOST PROPERTY

If you lose an item at one of the theme parks, first check with Guest Services

Public Holidays
Jan 1:
New Year's Day
Jan (third Mon):
Martin Luther
King Day
Feb (third Mon):
Presidents' Day
Mar/Apr: Good
Friday (optional)
May (last Mon):
Memorial Day
Jul 4:
Independence Day
Sept (first Mon):
Labor Day
Oct (second Mon):
Columbus Day
Nov 11:
Veterans' Day
Nov (last Thur):
Thanksgiving
Dec 25:
Christmas Day
NB: Boxing Day
(St Stephen's Day)
is not a public
holiday in the US.

who will direct you to the park's lost property office.

M

MAPS

Florida tourist offices (including overseas) often distribute the Official Transportation Map of Florida, which has city plans, free of charge. You'll also find a variety of free general maps showing main sections of the Orlando area at hotels, tourist centers, etc. The Insight Fleximap of Orlando is laminated and very practical.

MEDIA

Newspapers: The *Orlando Sentinel* is the city's daily newspaper. *Orlando Weekly*, published on Thursdays, is the region's alternative paper for news, opinion, arts, and entertainment. The national daily, *USA Today*, is distributed free at many hotels.

Magazines: The monthly *Orlando Magazine* has interesting feature articles on the arts, entertainment, dining, etc. A good source for monthly listings and information is *Where* magazine, distributed free at many hotels.

Radio: Highlights of Orlando's many stations include WMFE 90.7 (public radio for news, information, and classical music), WHTQ 96.5(classic rock), WCFB 94.5 (soul and R&B), WLOQ 103.1 (jazz), WDBO 580 (news, talk radio).

Television: Among the dozens of cable and terrestrial channels are Central Florida News 13 (Channel 13), WMFE-TV-PBS (Channel 24), WFTV-ABC (Channel 9), WKMG-CBS (Channel 6), WESH-NBC (Channel 2).

MONEY

Currency: The currency in the US is the dollar, divided into 100 cents. Coins come in denominations of 1 cent (penny), 5 cents (nickle), 10 cents (dime) and 25 cents (quarter). There are a limited number of 50-cent (half-dollar) and dollar coins in circulation. Dollar bills (notes) come in $1, $5, $10, $20, $50, $100, and $500.

Travelers' Checks: Foreign visitors are advised to take US dollar travelers' checks to Orlando, since exchanging foreign currency – whether as cash or checks – can prove problematic. An increasing number of banks, including the First Union National Bank, Nations Bank, and Sun Bank chains, offer foreign exchange facilities, but this practice is not universal. Some department stores offer foreign currency exchange.

Most shops, restaurants, and gas stations accept travelers' checks in US dollars and will give change in cash.

Cash Machines: The easiest way to take out money is from an ATM (automatic teller machine) with a debit or credit card using your PIN. Cash machines are widespread around the

Above from far left: checking the map; using an ATM is the easiest way to withdraw cash; dinky post office; clapboard church.

city. The most widely accepted cards are Visa, American Express, MasterCard, Diners Club, Japanese Credit Bureau, and Discover. Maestro cards are often not accepted.

Be sure to check the rate of exchange and any other charges your financial institution may levy before using your card abroad. Some charge prohibitive rates. The ATM operators will usually apply a charge as well, though you will be notified of this on-screen before you complete the transaction.

Credit Cards: Credit cards are very much part of daily life in Orlando and can be used to pay for almost everything. Car rental firms and hotels will usually take an imprint of your card as a deposit.

P

POST

Post Offices: The opening hours of post offices vary between central, big-city branches and those in smaller towns or suburbs, but all open Monday to Friday (generally 8 or 9am to 5pm) and some open on Saturday mornings. Drugstores and hotels usually have a small selection of stamps, and there are stamp-vending machines in some transport terminals. You can also print postage and labels online at http://www.usps.com.

Delivery Services: For the best service, you should pay for Express Mail via the US postal service, which

guarantees next-day delivery within the US and delivery within two to three days to foreign destinations. Privately owned courier services, which offer next-day delivery to most places, are also very popular. Telephone numbers for the main courier services are:
FedEx: 800-463-3339
DHL: 800-225-5435
UPS: 800-742-5877

R

RELIGION

Nearly every faith and denomination is represented in Orlando. Places of worship are listed in the telephone directory's Yellow Pages. Or try www.worshiporlando.org.

S

SMOKING

Smoking is not permitted in restaurants, most public buildings and areas, or at theme parks, though these have designated smoking areas. Hotels are predominantly non-smoking, though many have smoking rooms; specify your preference when booking.

T

TAXES

A Florida sales tax of 6.5 or 7 percent is added to all merchandise at the sales counter except for necessary medicine and grocery items. In addition, a

Parking
Parking costs $11 a day at Disney theme parks (free to WDW resort guests). Parking attendants will direct you to one of the many lots named after Disney characters. To avoid feeling Goofy or Dopey at the end of a long day, jot down the lot and row number to ensure you can find your car easily.

Tourist Development tax of between 2 and 6 percent is levied on hotel rooms. Both taxes vary by county.

TELEPHONES

Phone Numbers: US telephone numbers have a 3-digit area code followed by a 7-digit number. Area codes for the Orlando metro region are 407 and 321. You should dial all 10 digits when making a call. To call a number outside this area code, you should first dial '1'. These calls will incur long-distance charges. Toll-free numbers have the prefix 800, 888 or 866; dial a '1' when calling these numbers. Cell phone (mobile) numbers have the same 10 digits as regular phone numbers.

Calling from Abroad: To call Orlando from the UK, dial 00 (international code) + 1 (USA) + the area code and number. To call other countries from the USA, first dial the international code (011), then the country code: Australia 61, Germany 49, Ireland 353, New Zealand 64, UK 44. Dial Canadian numbers as you would a long-distance US number.

Public Telephones: Phone booths are common in public areas. They take coins and/or credit cards. You can also buy phone cards with prepaid minutes from convenience stores, service stations and other outlets, but be aware that there are often hidden charges when using them from public phone booths – read the fine print on the back for details.

TIME ZONES

Orlando is on Eastern Standard Time (EST). It is 5 hours behind Greenwich Mean time (GMT) and 3 hours ahead of Pacific Standard Time. It observes Daylight Saving Time (1 hour ahead) from mid-March through October.

TIPPING

Service personnel expect tips in Orlando. The accepted rate for baggage handlers in airports is at least $1 per bag. For others, including taxi drivers and waiters, 15–20 percent is the going rate, depending on the level and quality of service. Sometimes tips are included in restaurant bills when dining in groups.

Moderate hotel tipping is around 50 cents per bag or suitcase handled by porters or bellboys. You should tip a doorman if he holds your car or performs other services. Tip chamber staff if you stay several days.

TOUR OPERATORS

Gator Tours/Gray Line Orlando is Central Florida's largest sightseeing company. It offers a city tour of Orlando, half-day and full-day tours of the local area, tours to attractions, deep-sea fishing and other activities; www.gatortours.com, tel: 407-522-5911 or 1-800-537-0917.

Orlando Tours offers a huge variety of coach tours and activity tours, including airboat rides, animal and wildlife tours, boat tours, cruises visits

ORMATION ⓘ

to all the major attractions and bus trips to other Florida cities; www.orlando-tours.com; 1-800-303-5107.

All Orlando Tours has a long list of city tours and attractions, cruises and water tours, dinner shows and activity tours; www.allorlandotours.com; tel: 702-233-1627 or 1-866-868-7786.

Orlando Ghost Tours has a two-hour walking tour of haunted sites in Downtown Orlando, including a chance to conduct your own para-normal investigation using specialized equipment. Tours depart from Church Street Station; www.hauntedorlando.com; tel: 407-247-0452.

TOURIST INFORMATION

In Orlando: The Official Visitor Center, 8723 International Drive, Suite 101, Orlando, FL 32819; tel: 407-363-5872 or 800-551-0181; www.orlando info.com. It is located at the corner of I-Drive and Austrian Row and is open daily from 8.30am to 6.30pm. This is a good one-stop source for information about the area, where you can pick up free maps, brochures, buy discounted theme park and attractions tickets, and book hotels.

In the UK: For a free holiday planning kit, tel: 0800-018 67 60; or visit www.orlandoinfo.com/uk.

Regional Tourist Information
Kissimmee-St Cloud Convention & Visitors Bureau, Visitor Information Center, 1925 E Irlo Bronson Memorial Highway/US192; Kissimmee, FL 34744; tel: 407-944-2400 or 1-800 333 KISS (5477); Mon–Fri 8am–5pm; www.FloridaKiss.com.

Florida's Space Coast Office of Tourism, 430 Brevard Avenue, Cocoa Village, FL 32922; tel: 877-572-3224; www.space-coast.com.

Tampa Bay Visitor Information Center, 615 Channelside Drive, Suite 108A, Tampa, FL 33602; tel: 813-223-2752 or 1-800-448-2672; Mon–Sat 9.30am–5.30pm, Sun 11am–5pm; www.visittampabay.com.

TRANSPORTATION

Arrival
By Car: From the north, interstate highways I-95, I-75 and I-10 bring you into Florida. They connect with I-4, US 192, Highway 528, and the Florida Turnpike which run through the Orlando metro area. From the south, Orlando is reached via I-75, I-95 and the Florida Turnpike.

By Bus: Greyhound (tel: 800-231-2222; www.greyhound.com) provides bus services to Florida and all over the state. While some intercity bus services include many stops en route, making long distances seem inter-minable, there are also express buses which take in fewer stops.

Many bus terminals, including the one in Downtown Orlando, are in a dodgy area of town, so take care when traveling to or from stations.

By Rail: Amtrak (tel: 800-872-7245; www.amtrak.com) offers slow and

Above from far left: Tampa Bay trips; stylish sign for the tourist information office; transport the kids will love.

Disney Information
www.disneyworld.com; Walt Disney World Guest Information, Box 10040, Lake Buena Vista, FL 32830-0040.
General park information: 407-824-4321 (automated) or 407-824-2222.
Disney vacation packages: 407-939-7675.
Park tours: 407-WDW-TOUR (407-939-8687).
Restaurant reservations: 407-WDW-DINE (407-939-3463).

leisurely services from America's Midwest, northeast, and south – and connecting service from points west – to certain Florida cities. There is a daily service between New York City and Miami on the Silver Service, with stops at Downtown Orlando, Kissimmee, Winter Park and Sanford. The Sunset Limited travels triweekly from Los Angeles via New Orleans. For those who want to take their car along, too, Amtrak offers an Auto Train service from Lorton, Virginia (near Washington DC), to Sanford.

By Air: Most major US and international carriers serve Orlando. Fare prices are competitive, so shop around before buying a ticket. A variety of discount fares and package deals, which can significantly cut round-trip rates, are also available. The many scheduled services are supplemented by charter flights.

Airports

Orlando International Airport: International airlines fly direct or via other US cities into Orlando International Airport, 9 miles (14km) south of Downtown Orlando and about 25 miles (40km) from Walt Disney World Resort. Spacious and glittering, it has three terminals, with satellite gates reached by 'peoplemover' shuttle trains. Disney characters often make appearances during the day. Tel: 407-825-2001 (general inquiries), 407-825-8463 (flight information).

Local buses depart from the A side of the Main Terminal on Level 1. Lynx buses 11 and 51 serve Downtown

Orlando; travel time is approximately 40 minutes. Lynx bus 42 serves International Drive; travel time is around 60 minutes. Fares are $1.75.

Taxis are located on both the A and B sides of the Main Terminal at the Ground Transportation Level (level 1). Metered rates vary, but fares range from $35 to Downtown, $33–39 to International Drive, $43–60 to Kissimmee and $60 to Walt Disney World.

Shuttle vans also operate from this location; fares per person range from $11–44, depending on the destination. All the major car rental firms have facilities at the airport.

Orlando Sanford Airport: Most vacation charter flights arrive at Sanford Airport, about 30 miles (48km) north of Orlando. During the busy summer months this small airport is utilized to cope with the large numbers of tourists, and lines at immigration can be long. Though it's conveniently located off I-4, the extra distance can be costly if you plan to use taxi or shuttle buses to reach Orlando. The major car rental firms are represented at the airport. Tel: 407-585-4000.

Transport within Orlando

Bus: The Orlando metro area has an excellent public bus system, called Lynx. It serves most of the popular theme parks, attractions, and shopping malls as well as the airports. Bus stops are marked in pink with the paw print of a lynx cat or a bus.

A single fare is $1.75. An all-day pass costs $4. You can buy both from

the bus driver, but exact change is required. Seven-day and 30-day passes for unlimited rides are also available from the visitor center *(see p. 105)*.

Lynx runs every day, though some schedules change or don't run on Sundays and holidays. Schedules are available at the visitor center or online at www.golynx.com. For more information contact customer service on tel: 407-841-5969.

The Lymmo bus system in Downtown Orlando provides free transportation from the T.D. Waterhouse Center to City Hall. There are 11 stations and 8 bus stops.

I-Ride Trolley: These cheery green trolleys run to all the attractions, hotels, and shopping malls along International Drive, from Prime Outlets south to Premium Outlets. They operate daily 8am–10.30pm. Single fares are $1, and exact change is required. Children under 12 ride free. You can also buy passes for unlimited rides for 1, 3, 5, 7 or 14 days, costing from $3 to $16, from a number of outlets. For information, tel: 407-354-5656; www.iridetrolley.com.

Taxis: Cabs are plentiful throughout the Orlando area, but they aren't cheap and you need to phone in advance for pick-up. Your hotel can do this for you, or there are several companies listed in the phone directory. For Yellow/City Cab, tel: 407 422-2222.

Car Rental: Renting a car is by far the easiest way to explore the Orlando area, allowing you to zip quickly between the major parks and attractions, unless, of course, you encounter one of the many traffic jams that snarl the area's major roads. If possible, avoid driving the I-4 corridor during rush hour (7–10am and 4–7pm).

Most rental agencies require that you are at least 21 years old (sometimes 25), have a valid driver's license and a major credit card. Some will take a cash deposit in lieu of a credit card, but this might be as high as $500.

Travelers from some foreign countries may need to produce an international driver's license from their own country. If you happen to book your car online in another country, you must provide a foreign driver's license for the discounted fee to be honored when you pick up the car.

Visitors wishing to rent a car after arriving in Orlando will find rental offices at the airports, at downtown locations, and even at some hotels. Rates are cheap by US and international standards, but you should shop around for the best rates and features. Local rental firms outside the airports are often less expensive than the national companies, and can be more convenient if you want a car only for a day or two. The cost of insurance is usually tacked on to the rental fee, so be sure to check insurance provisions before signing anything.

If you are traveling from overseas, it is normally cheaper to arrange car rental in advance. You should also check with your airline or travel agent for special package deals that include a

Above from far left: old-fashioned transportation; literal railroad crossing; Disney mobile; I-Ride Trolley.

SCRUB JAY XING

Car-Hire Agencies
These agencies may be contacted within the US and from abroad:
• Alamo
Tel: 800-462-5266; www.alamo.com.
• Avis
US: tel: 800-331-1212; www.avis.com; UK: tel: 0844-581-8181; www.avis.co.uk.
• Budget
US: tel: 800-527-0700; UK: tel: 01344-484-100; www.drivebudget.com.
• Dollar
US: tel: 800-800-3665; UK: tel: 0808-234-7524; www.dollar.com.
• Hertz
US: tel: 800-654-3131; www.hertz.com; UK: tel: 0870-844-8844; www.hertz.co.uk
• National
US: tel: 800-227-7368; UK tel: 0870-400-4581; www.nationalcar.com.
• Thrifty
US: tel: 800-847-4389; www.thrifty.com.

car, since rental rates can be reduced by about 50 percent if you buy a so-called 'fly-drive' deal. However, be wary of offers of 'free' car rental, which do not include extras like tax and insurance.

Be sure to check that your car-rental agreement includes Loss Damage Waiver (LDW), also known as Collision Damage Waiver (CDW). Without it, you will be liable for any damage done to your vehicle in the event of an accident, regardless of whether or not you were to blame. You are advised to pay for supplementary Liability Insurance on top of the standard third-party insurance. Insurance and tax charges combined can add $35 to each day's rental – as much as the fee for the car itself. US drivers can normally use their personal car insurance to cover a rental vehicle.

Driving
Getting around Orlando by car is generally easy, though traffic is heavy on some routes. Road signage is good and exits for major attractions and areas are well marked.

Toll Roads: There are several toll roads in Orlando, with tolls ranging from 75 cents to $1.50 for various portions of the road. It is often worth it to use the toll roads because they are generally quicker and save you time sitting in traffic jams on other busy roads. The airport access roads are also toll roads. You do not have to have exact change. Use the lane marked 'Change and Receipts' where there is an attendant. Do not make the mistake

of using the 'SunPass Only' lane – this is for prepaid tolls only and you will receive a hefty fine if you drive through it without one.

Rules of the Road: Driving is on the right. You must carry your driving license at all times or you can be fined. Unless there is a sign prohibiting it, you can turn right on a red light after making a complete stop and checking that the way is clear. On a two-way street, cars traveling in both directions must stop for a school bus with its lights flashing and remain stopped until the bus drives off (this does not apply to a divided highway).

Seatbelts: These must be worn at all times by drivers and front-seat passengers. Children age 4 and under, and those weighing less than 40 pounds (18 kg), must be placed in an approved child safety seat. These should be available for a fee from car rental agencies, or for information on obtaining one, tel: 1-877-543-7328, www.buckleupflorida.com.

Alcohol: Florida has some of the toughest laws in the US against driving under the influence of alcohol, including jail, automatic loss of your license, and stiff fines. The maximum level permitted is so small that you are advised to drink no alcohol at all if driving. It is also illegal to have an open container of alcohol in your vehicle.

Speed Limits: American states set their own speed limits. In Florida

they are: 55–70mph (85–110kmh) on highways, 20–30mph (30–45kmh) in residential areas, 15mph (20kmh) near schools. Limits change suddenly and for only short distances, so pay attention to signs. The Highway Patrol is good at enforcing limits, including minimum speeds: signs along interstates sometimes oblige motorists to drive at over 40mph (65kmh).

Gas (petrol): Fuel is sold in American gallons and comes in three grades of unleaded gasoline. Most self-service pumps are automatic and accept credit and debit cards, or you will have to pre-pay inside. Prices vary considerably between different service stations; many are open 24 hours.

Parking: All of the theme parks charge hefty parking fees, but parking is free at shopping malls, many museums, and other attractions. Street parking is limited in Downtown Orlando; it is best to use the parking garages. Look for signs indicating parking restrictions and tow-away zones. Park in the same direction as the flow of traffic, and do not park on the curb.

V

VISAS AND PASSPORTS

Most foreign visitors need a machine-readable passport (which should be valid for at least six months longer than their intended stay) and a visa to enter the US. You should also be able to provide evidence that you intend to leave the US after your visit is over (usually in the form of a return or onward ticket), and visitors from some countries need an international vaccination certificate.

Certain foreign nationals are exempt from the normal visa requirements. Canadian citizens with a valid Canadian passport need no visa. Nor do Mexican citizens provided they have a Mexican passport as well as a US Border Crossing Card (Form I-186 or I-586), and as long as they are residents of Mexico.

Under the 'visa-waiver' program, citizens of 27 countries do not require a visa if they are staying for less than 90 days and have a round-trip or onward ticket. These include the UK, Ireland, Australia, New Zealand, Japan, France, and Germany. If you travel under this program, you will need to present an e-passport if your passport was assigned on or after 26 October 2006.

Mistakes are not accepted on immigration forms you fill in during the flight. So don't cross anything out – ask for a new form.

Those requiring a visa or visa information can apply by mail or by personal application to their local US Embassy or Consulate.

W

WEIGHTS AND MEASURES

The imperial system is used in the US. Metric weights and measures are rarely used.

Above from far left: take care where you cross the road: jaywalking is an offence in most urban areas in the US; a bumpy, wet ride.

Traffic Conditions I-4 can become heavily congested, especially during rush hour. For current traffic conditions, dial 511 (or check online at www.FL511.com); this is the Florida Department of Transportation's free hotline for up-to-date traffic information, construction and severe weather reports on all Florida interstate highways including I-4.

With nearly 450 hotels and more than 112,000 guest rooms, Orlando has a wealth of lodging options. Accommodations range from luxury resorts and themed hotels to charming bed and breakfasts, economy hotels/motels, and campgrounds. There are also more than 26,000 vacation home rentals available and more than 16,000 vacation ownership units. Although standards for services and facilities are generally quite high, there is the occasional bad apple. Some of the cheapest accommodations offered by tour operators are positively miserable, so be sure you know what you're getting into before signing on the dotted line. If you're staying at Disney spend the extra money to stay at a resort they classify as Moderate or Deluxe – the attention to detail at these resorts guarantees a magical vacation.

Reservations and Prices

Reservations are generally required, and if you are traveling during the high season you should book several months ahead if you have your heart set on a particular hotel or if you want to stay inside Walt Disney World Resort.

Room rates vary enormously between high season and low season *(see margin, right)*. There is plenty of scope to ask for a discount if you are staying for a week or more, or if you are visiting during the off-season, which for many hotels is a lean time.

Florida also imposes a resort tax, in addition to the usual sales tax, which is added to the price of all hotel rooms. It varies from county to county and ranges from between 2 and 5 percent.

Walt Disney World Resort

All-Star Movies, Music, and Sports

1991 West Buena Vista Drive, Lake Buena Vista; tel: 407-939 7000 (All-Star Movies), 407-939 6000 (All-Star Music), 407-939 5000 (All-Star Sports); $$

This is one of only two budget Disney complexes. It has 30 three-story buildings divided by themes. Each has a distinctive facade, but aside from a few decorative touches, the size and decor of most rooms are identical: they're 260 sq ft (24 sq meters), have two double beds, small bureaus, a table with chairs, and bathrooms with separate vanity areas. Popular with families, the resort has a game room, playground, outdoor pool, shopping, and food court. Buses transport guests to the parks.

Boardwalk Resort and Villas

2101 Epcot Resorts Boulevard, Lake Buena Vista; tel: 407-939-5100; $$$

Elaborately detailed buildings with turreted, brightly colored facades and twinkling lights which recreate an East Coast boardwalk circa 1920. Spacious rooms with ocean-blue and sea-green furnishings have two queen-size brass

Price for a standard double room for one night without breakfast:

$$$	over US$200
$$	US$110–200
$	under US$110

beds, daybeds, and ceiling fans; two-story garden suites have private gardens. The villas – Disney Vacation Club timeshare units – sleep 4 to 12 and have kitchens, laundries, whirlpool tubs, and internet access. Nightclubs, restaurants, midway games, and shops line the boardwalk. There's a super-vised evening children's program, a health club, a large swimming pool with a 200-ft (60-meter) water slide, and boat transportation to Epcot.

Buena Vista Palace

1900 Buena Vista Drive, Lake Buena Vista; tel: 866-397-6516; www.buenavistapalace.com; $$

Located across the lagoon from Downtown Disney, the Palace's rooms are all very well appointed in sleek modern furnishings and pillow-top beds. Most have outdoor balconies, and some even offer a view of the lake. The Island Suites provide more space than the smallish rooms. The resort has large spa and pool facilities and six restaurants to choose from.

Grand Floridian Resort and Spa

4401 Grand Floridian Way, Lake Buena Vista; tel: 407-824-3000; $$$

The Victorian era in all its splendor is recreated at Disney's flagship prop-erty, an elegant confection of glistening white, wooden buildings with red-shingled roofs, gracious verandas and turrets. Open-cage elevators in the plant-filled, five-story, chandeliered lobby serve second-floor shops and restaurants. Most rooms in the four-

and five-story lodge buildings have two queen-size beds and a daybed; many overlook the Seven Seas Lagoon. Amenities include some of Disney's finest dining experiences at Victoria and Albert's and Citricos, and a fine waterside restaurant, Nar-coossee's; several bars, a supervised evening children's program, the Grand Floridian Health Club and Spa, three swimming pools, and water activities. Monorail to Epcot and Magic Kingdom, boat to Magic Kingdom.

Polynesian Resort

1600 Seven Seas Drive, Lake Buena Vista; tel: 407-824-2000; $$$

One of Disney's most authentic theme hotels recreates a Pacific Island retreat. The centerpiece is the Great Ceremo-nial House, a tropical extravaganza of plants and waterfalls. Rooms, in 11 two- and three-story 'longhouses,' vary in size, but most have two queen-size beds, a daybed, and balconies. Those overlooking the Seven Seas Lagoon afford front-row seats for Magic Kingdom fireworks. There are several restaurants and bars, two pools, a play-ground, supervised evening children's programs, and water activities. Mono-rail to Magic Kingdom and Epcot, boat to Magic Kingdom.

Universal Orlando Resort
Hard Rock Hotel

5800 Universal Boulevard, Orlando; tel: 407-503-2000; $$$

Not quite as lavish or expensive as the Portofino, the accommodations at this Mission-style hotel range from very

Above from far left: sunbathing on the beach of the Seven Seas lagoon; the elegant facade of the Grand Floridian hotel.

High and Low Seasons
Orlando hotel prices vary quite dramatically between the seasons, which are unsurprisingly linked to the US school calendar. The Christmas break period (mid–December until New Year) is the most expensive, followed by spring break (mid-February until the end of March) and summer (end of May until the beginning of August). The cheapest times to visit are from New Year until mid-February, August and September (but be prepared for extraordinary heat), and the first half of December.

Universal Perks
Free water taxis transport guests between the theme parks and the three Universal hotels. Best of all, guests at all on-site hotels are given Express access to nearly all rides and attractions.

comfortable standard rooms to large and opulent suites. An eclectic array of rock 'n' roll memorabilia is displayed tastefully around the building, which nearly surrounds a huge pool with a sandy beach, water slide, and underwater sound system. Several restaurants and bars, a fitness room, an indoor play area, and a Hard Rock store round out the picture.

Portofino Bay Hotel

5601 Universal Boulevard, Orlando; tel: 407-503-1000; $$$

This is such a beautifully designed and constructed re-creation of the real Portofino, you'd be forgiven for calling out *buon giorno* from your window first thing in the morning, especially after that first cup of stiff Italian coffee. Set on a harbor filled with fishing boats, the hotel offers some of the most luxurious accommodations in Orlando, with large, sumptuous rooms, three elaborate pools, a spa, an indoor children's play area, and several restaurants, including the elegant Delfino Riviera. Very expensive, but worth it.

Royal Pacific Resort

6300 Hollywood Way, Orlando; tel: 407-503-3000; $$$

Attempting to recreate the South Pacific in central Florida, this resort is centered around a lagoon-like pool fringed with palm trees, waterfalls, a sandy beach, and cabanas. Accommodations are priced slightly lower than the Hard Rock Hotel but sacrifice little in the way of comfort and amenities, which include six restaurants and bars, a children's activity room, a fitness room, and convention facilities.

Downtown Orlando

Eö Inn

227 North Eola Drive, Orlando; tel: 407-481-8485; www.eoinn.com; $$$

This historic inn was built in 1923 and overlooks Lake Eola in the prestigious Thornton Park area. It was converted into a fine boutique hotel in 1999. With only 17 rooms, the service is always personable, and the decor is chic and spacious. On site is the Urban Spa, a perfect spot for some serious pampering.

Grand Bohemian Hotel

325 South Orange Avenue, Orlando; tel: 407-313-9000 or 1-866-663-0024; www.GrandBohemianHotel.com; $$$

This high-style hotel, across from City Hall, is itself a masterpiece, with more than 100 pieces of rare artwork *(see p.61)*, including drawings by Gustav Klimt and Egon Schiele. The Bösendorfer Lounge offers nightly entertainment on one of only two Imperial Grand Bösendorfer pianos in the world. The 250 guest rooms and

Price for a standard double room for one night without breakfast:

$$$ over US$200
$$ US$110–200
$ under US$110

suites are dramatically furnished in dark Java wood tones, soft red and purple velvet fabrics, silver paint, Tiffany-style lamps, and the luxurious all-white 'heavenly bed'. All rooms have CD players, high-speed internet access, and interactive TV. The elegant, four-star Boheme Restaurant *(see p.119)* attracts Downtown's business and arts community. Other amenities include a heated outdoor pool, spa, massage room, workout room, and guest privileges at nearby Citrus Athletic Club.

Veranda Bed & Breakfast

115 North Summerlin Avenue, Orlando; tel: 407-849-0321 or 800-420-6822; www.theveranda bandb.com; $$

Five cozy 1920s homes in Downtown Orlando have been turned into this delightful B&B. All the rooms have hardwood floors and lovely period furnishings. You couldn't find an experience further away from the anonymous chain hotels lining US 192 and I-Drive.

International Drive

DoubleTree Castle Hotel

8629 International Drive, Orlando; tel: 407-345-1511; www.double treecastle.com; $$

Spires, mosaics, banners, and rich purple-and-gold drapes and bedspreads give this mid-range hotel a touch of medieval whimsy. The freshly baked Doubletree chocolate chip cookies on arrival are a welcoming touch. Amenities include two restau-

rants, a fitness center, free shuttles to the theme parks, and a pleasant heated courtyard pool.

Enclave Suites at Orlando

6165 Carrier Drive, Orlando; tel: 407-351-1155 or 800-457-0077; www.enclavesuites.com; $$

Located just off International Drive, this all-suites hotel offers a lot more than the average chain. All the rooms include a fully-fitted kitchen, and the Kid Suites are decorated in theme-park style. There are two outdoor pools and one indoor pool, as well as two kiddie pools and a playground to keep everyone busy.

Fairfield Inn and Suites Orlando International Drive

7495 Canada Avenue, Orlando; tel: 407-351-7000; $

Operated by Marriott, this Universal and SeaWorld partner hotel is located just off I-Drive and is convenient for the theme parks and other attractions. Its 200 spacious guest rooms have free high-speed internet access, work desk, and cable TV. Suites have separate seating area, mini-refrigerator, and microwave. Outdoor heated pool, whirlpool, and fitness room.

International Plaza Resort & Spa

10100 International Drive, Orlando; tel: 407-352-1100 or 1-800-327-0363; www.IntlPlazaResort.com; $$

Located across the street from SeaWorld and Aquatica, this beautifully renovated hotel covers 28 acres (11

Above from far left: arriving in style at Portofino Bay; the Velvet Room at the Hard Rock Hotel; Castle Hotel.

Hidden Charges
Don't forget to check the hidden charges when booking a hotel. All hotels add a bed tax, which varies from county to county and can be as high as 5 percent. Also, do not make any in-room calls until you check the rates (these should be provided near the phone). Local and toll-free calls are usually free, but not always; and when they are not, they usually cost much, much more than they should.

hectares). Its 1,100 rooms and suites are set around central gardens or in the executive tower. The finest rooms have a Balinese-inspired decor, with luxurious fittings in native dark wood and bamboo, and tranquil blue and green soft furnishings. Guests can relax around one of the three palm-lined pools, in quiet corners of the garden or in L'Esprit Day Spa. Other amenities include a miniature golf course (coming soon), complimentary wireless internet access, deli, and pool bar.

The Peabody Orlando

9801 International Drive, Orlando; tel: 407-352-4000 or 800-732-2639; www.peabodyorlando.com; $$$

This 27-story landmark hotel in the tourist corridor has an Olympic-size pool and takes pride in being Orlando's convention hotel of choice. Though known for its twice-daily 'March of the Peabody Ducks,' this is not really a place for kids. Guests looking for high tea and fine room service will feel more at home.

Rosen Shingle Creek

9939 Universal Boulevard, Orlando; tel: 407-996-9939 or 1-866-996-9939; www.RosenShingleCreek.com; $$-$$$

> Price for a standard double room for one night without breakfast:
>
> $$$ over US$200
> $$ US$110–200
> $ under US$110

You could almost forget that this gorgeous hotel is right in the heart of Orlando just a mile (1.5km) from the Convention Center. Set back from the main roads on 230 acres (93 hectares), it has an 18-hole championship golf course; tennis courts; a lap pool, family pool and quiet pool surrounded by pretty gardens; and a nature trail alongside cypress-lined Shingle Creek. The 1,500 guestrooms and suites have luxurious furnishings in soft earth tones, large-screen TVs and many amenities. The VIP Concierge Lounge offers further amenities. Relaxing body and beauty treatments are available at The Spa. And there are 12 restaurants and bars to choose from, including Cala Bella, a fine-dining Italian bistro, and A Land Remembered steakhouse *(see p.120)*.

Kissimmee and Celebration

ALL STAR Vacation Homes

7822 West Irlo Bronson Memorial Highway (Hwy 192), Kissimmee; tel: 407-997-0733 or 1-800-592-5568; www.allstarvacationhomes.com; $$-$$$

This leading property management company has more than 150 fully furnished vacation home rentals within 4 miles (6km) of Walt Disney World, ranging from 2- and 3-bedroom condos to fabulous 7-bedroom town homes with private pools. Other amenities include spas, game rooms, home movie theaters and high-speed internet access, with TVs and DVD players in every bedroom. The homes

are beautifully decorated, well-located and maintained, and a great alternative to traditional hotels, especially for longer stays.

Clarion Resort and Waterpark

2261 E. Irlo Bronson Memorial Hwy, Kissimmee; tel: 407-846-2221 or 1-866-975-4337; http://clarionwaterpark.com/index.shtml; $–$$

With guestrooms cheerfully decorated in bright tropical colors, this hotel offers great amenities for a family vacation. A mini-waterpark occupies the central courtyard, with three large water slides for all ages, kiddie slides, a lazy river, two pools and spa area. There is a teen activity area and children's playroom. Couples are catered for with in-room jacuzzi suites. Rooms have complimentary wireless internet, desk, cable TV, CD/MP3 player and a kitchenette. At the east end of Highway 192, the hotel is just 5 minutes from the Silver Spurs Rodeo Arena, and also has easy access to Disney theme parks via the Osceola Parkway.

Galleria Palms Hotel and Suites

3000 Maingate Lane, off Hwy 192, Kissimmee; tel: 407-396-6300 or 1-800-391-7909; www.galleriapalmsorlando.com; $

A short drive from Walt Disney World, this hotel is incredibly good value, with many extras normally found at higher priced hotels. Located

west of I-4, it's set back half a block off Highway 192, making it surprisingly quiet for such a convenient location on the main drag. Rooms are well appointed in restful beige and brown tones, with wet bar, microwave, refrigerator and cable TV. Complimentary in-room wireless internet, Bath and Body Works toiletries, deluxe continental breakfast and an outdoor pool round out the amenities.

Ginn Reunion Resort

1000 Reunion Way, Reunion; tel: 407-662-1100 or 1-888-418-9611; www.GinnReunionResort.com; $$$

With three signature golf courses designed by leading golf pros, a tennis center, spa, water park and miles of biking and walking trails, there's something for every member of the family at this upscale, luxury resort. It covers 2,300 acres (930 hectares) in a newly-developed area 6 miles (9.5km) south of Walt Disney World. Accommodations range from luxury suites in the Reunion Grande to villas overlooking the golf course to private homes. There is fine dining at the Forte Restaurant and tapas-style food and great views at Eleven, the rooftop lounge.

Holiday Inn Main Gate East

5711 West US Hwy 192, Kissimmee; tel: 407-396-4222 or 1-800-327-1128; www.holidayinnmge.com; $–$$

Across the road from Old Town and just 3 miles (2km) from Disney, this spacious hotel offers many family facilities and great value. Its 444

Above from far left: time out by the pool; looking on to the hotel golf course; the balconies are big at this Florida hotel.

Camping Out

Fort Wilderness Resort within Walt Disney World Resort has more than 800 campsites for tents and RVs. Another option is to rent a trailer (decked out like a log cabin) that sleeps up to six people and has air conditioning, color TV, radio, cookware, and linen, i.e. all the equipment you'll need. The resort is located amid 650 acres (260 hectares) of woods and streams on Bay Lake, east of the Magic Kingdom. For information and reservations, tel: 407-824-2900.

Booking Disney
Information on all
of Disney's resort
hotels can be found
at www.disney
world.com.
Reservations can
be made there or
by phoning tel: 407-
939-7429 (room
only) or 407-939-
7675 (vacation
packages).
All Disney's resorts
are connected to all
Disney's parks by
bus. Some resorts
are connected to
individual parks by
monorail or boat – a
great way to arrive.

rooms are decorated in bright, bold colors, with private balconies and free high-speed internet access. Upgraded rooms include kid suites, king bedrooms with added work space, and a fabulous two-room VIP suite with jetted bathtub, granite bar and full-size kitchenette. Amenities include a large outdoor heated pool, separate kids' pool, kids' theater and games room, fitness center, lounge bar and Trattoria food court.

Terrace Hotel

329 East Main Street, Lakeland;
tel: 863-688-0800 or
1 888-644-8400;
www.terracehotel.com; $$

This luxury hotel in pretty, downtown Lakeland is a good place to stop after a visit to Cypress Gardens or en route to Tampa Bay, and makes a nice change from the busier cities without costing you an arm and a leg. Built in the 1920s, it retains lovely period architecture in the Terrace Grille restaurant *(see p.121)* with high French windows overlooking Lake Mirror. The 73 rooms are stylishly decorated with beautiful, contemporary furnishings. They include free high-speed internet, cable TV and several restful amenities.

> Price for a standard
> double room for one
> night without breakfast:
>
> $$$ over US$200
> $$ US$110–200
> $ under US$110

Winter Park and Maitland

Park Plaza Hotel

307 Park Avenue South,
Winter Park; tel: 407-647-1072 or
1-800-228-7220;
www.parkplazahotel.com; $$–$$$

From its wood-paneled lobby to the wicker armchairs on the fern-filled, wrought-iron balconies overlooking Park Avenue, this hotel exudes old-fashioned charm. Built in 1921, it is a landmark in the heart of Winter Park's main shopping and dining area. Antiques grace the lobby and guestrooms, where wooden floors, ceiling fans and brass beds add to the ambience. The acclaimed Park Plaza Gardens restaurant *(see p.122)* offers fine dining in a delightful indoor garden setting.

Thurston House Bed and Breakfast

851 Lake Avenue,
Maitland; tel: 407-539-1911 or
800-843-2721;
www.thurstonhouse.com; $$

Set on the shores of Lake Eulalia, this pretty Victorian farmhouse is a reminder of days long gone in central Florida. One thing that hasn't changed is the fact that you can still sit in a rocking chair on the veranda and watch the osprey dive for fish in the lake. Built in 1885 and restored in 1991, this bed and breakfast combines all the charm of a Victorian inn with the modern amenities you would expect in a small hotel – plus some you wouldn't, like original fireplaces filled with candles.

The Space Coast

The Inn at Cocoa Beach

4300 Ocean Beach Boulevard, Cocoa Beach; tel: 321-799-3460 or 1-800-343-5307; www.theinnatcocoabeach.com; $$–$$$

Gracious and welcoming, this pretty oceanside hotel is a perfect combination of old-fashioned Southern charm and laid-back beach lifestyle. Rooms are individually and tastefully decorated, some with four-poster beds, jacuzzis or French country furniture. All have ocean views. Deluxe rooms have separate sitting areas and private balconies facing the sea, while standard rooms also overlook the large pool. Guests enjoy a scrumptious home-baked breakfast on the patio, an evening wine and cheese social, and an honors bar in the library. The beach is just through the garden gate, and there's even a colorful parrot for company.

Ron Jon Resort

1000 Shorewood Drive, Cape Canaveral; tel: 866-854-4835; www.ronjonresort.com; $$

Ron Jon has two quirky advantages: it is the closest oceanfront resort to most Orlando attractions, and it is the nearest place outside the Kennedy Space Center to watch a launch. This property is primarily for timeshare owners, but its unique location makes it well worth checking out for a night or two on the coast. Kids will love the elaborate pools, lazy river, and water slide. The suites aren't big but they are comfortable.

Tampa Bay

Hampton Inn & Suites

1301 E. 7th Avenue, Tampa; tel: 813-247-6700; www.tampaybocity suites.hamptoninn.com; $$

Right in the heart of Ybor City's historic district, this comfortable hotel is a great base for enjoying the district's famous nightlife, and is also convenient for downtown Tampa attractions. Rooms and suites are attractively decorated and have complimentary high-speed internet, refrigerators, and many other amenities. Some have jacuzzi spa tubs. A hot breakfast bar is included in the rate, and there's also an outdoor pool and fitness center.

Seminole Hard Rock Hotel & Casino

5223 North Orient Road, Tampa; tel: 813-627-7625 or 1-866-502-7529; www.seminolehardrock.com; $$$

Owned and run by the Seminole tribe, this Hard Rock Hotel is the hottest place to stay in Tampa. The gleaming white tower with its 50-foot (15-meter) Hard Rock guitar in front is visible from miles away. The 24-hour casino is chock full of memorabilia from rock 'n' roll legends; some items have touch-screens for background history and music videos. Rooms are large and very chic, decorated in relaxing shades of mint green, silver and white. A beautiful pool with cabanas, several good restaurants, the Whammy Bar and a full-service spa and fitness center provide more places to play.

Above from far left: palatial hotel; close attention to detail; music-themed sign and decor at the super-hip Seminole Hard Rock Hotel & Casino.

Theme Park Transportation

There is hardly a hotel or motel in central Florida that does not list 'free transportation to Disney' as one of its amenities, but the services most provide are very limited, with one departure and one return from each park per day. The timings are often inconvenient too, meaning you'll miss the quieter morning hours and the evening shows and fireworks. Don't count on it for a flexible vacation, especially with children.

Walt Disney World Resort

Bongos Cuban Café

1498 East Buena Vista Drive, Downtown Disney; tel: 407-828-0999; Sun–Thu 11am–11pm, Fri–Sat 11am–midnight; live music Fri–Sat 9pm–2am; $$

Old Havana meets Miami's South Beach in this stylish restaurant owned by superstar Gloria Estefan and her husband Emilio. The building is shaped like an enormous pineapple, with tropical deco design and hand-painted murals of 1940s Cuba inside. The Cuban dishes feature seafood, chicken, steak and pork, served with plantains and other Caribbean accompaniments. Live music and dancing at the weekends.

Chefs de France

Epcot World Showcase, France Pavilion; tel: 407-939-3463; daily lunch and dinner; $$

The more accessible of France's two restaurants, there is nothing pretentious in this restaurant's decor – a faithful re-creation of a typical Parisian café. The cooking may not be up to Michelin-star status, but it is very good, and you get the opportunity to dine under a faux Eiffel Tower.

Price guide for a two-course dinner for one with half a bottle of house wine, not including tax and tip:

$$$	above US$50
$$	US$25–50
$	below US$25

Coral Reef Restaurant

Epcot Future World, The Seas with Nemo and Friends; 407-939-3463; daily lunch and dinner; $$$

This seafood restaurant, alongside the aquarium at The Seas with Nemo and Friends, provides dreamy views into the largest inland saltwater environment ever built, which contains 85 different species of tropical fish. The food is fine dining at Disney's best, and it's hard to beat the setting.

House of Blues

1490 East Buena Vista Drive, Downtown Disney; tel: 407-934-2583; www.hob.com/orlando; daily 11am–late; $$

Founded by original Blues Brother Dan Aykroyd and others, and done up like a ramshackle wharfside warehouse in the Mississippi Delta. The food is surprisingly good for a chain operation, with spicy southern favorites like fried catfish, seafood gumbo, jambalaya, and bread pudding dribbled with brandy sauce. And there's free live music in the restaurant Thursday–Saturday from 10.30pm till closing time.

Universal Orlando Resort

Emeril's Restaurant Orlando

6000 Universal Boulevard, CityWalk, tel: 407-224-2424; www.emerils.com; daily 11.30am–2pm and Sun–Thu 5.30–10pm, Fri–Sat 5.30–11pm; $$$

This sophisticated restaurant features the creations of celebrity chef Emeril Lagasse. Assertive Creole flavors bubble up through artfully prepared specialties like grilled pork chop with-

caramelized sweet potatoes. The wine connoisseurs can choose from more than 10,000 bottles. The desserts are equally glorious as homey favorites like root beer float and banana cream pie become decadent masterpieces.

Hard Rock Café Orlando

6050 Universal Boulevard; tel: 407-351-7625; www.hardrock.com; daily 11am–late; $$

When it comes to theme restaurants, this is the big daddy of 'em all. The largest Hard Rock Café in the world, the walls here are plastered with gold records, album covers, flashy costumes, and instruments that have been strummed and drummed by some of the rock world's biggest names. Aretha Franklin's pink Cadillac revolves over the bar. The menu ranges from its legendary burgers to hickory smoked barbecue, but save room for the hot fudge brownie sundae. Free tours are available in the afternoons.

Jimmy Buffet's Margaritaville

6000 Universal Boulevard, CityWalk; tel: 407-224-2155; www.margarita villeorlando.com; daily 11am–2am; $$

The famous Margaritas are accompanied by a tasty range of Floribbean fare, whether you're in the mood for a cheeseburger in paradise, coconut shrimp, jerk salmon or Jimmy's jammin' jambalaya. Enjoy them outdoors on the Porch of Indecision, or at the waterfront tiki bar alongside Jimmy's own seaplane. After dinner the restaurant becomes a nightclub with live music nightly.

Mythos

Islands of Adventure, Lost Continent; tel: 407-224-4012; daily lunch and dinner; $$$

The park's best restaurant is ensconced in a regally appointed cavern with sculpted walls, purple upholstery, and lagoon views. Entrées include wood-roasted lobster with wild mushroom risotto, cedar-planked salmon with orange horseradish mashed potatoes, and wood-fired pizza.

The Boheme

Grand Bohemian Hotel, 325 South Orange Avenue, Orlando; tel: 407-313-9000; www.theboheme.com; daily 6am–2.30pm, Sun 6am–10.30am, Sun–Thur 5–10.30pm, Fri–Sat 5–11.30pm; $$$

This is one of Orlando's best restaurants, the scene of power breakfasts, elegant lunches and intimate dinners. Paintings from the hotel's superb art collection grace the walls. The menu features nouvelle cuisine with Pacific Rim, French and Italian accents. Reservations are recommended for the superb Sunday jazz brunch, when some of Florida's hottest musicians play.

Ceviche Tapas Bar and Restaurant

125 W. Church Street; tel: 321-281-8140; www.ceviche.com; Tue–Thur 5pm–midnight, Fri–Sat 5pm–1am; flamenco room Thur–Sat 5pm–2am; $–$$

Over 100 hot and cold tapas from Catalonia and northern Spain, along with

Above from far left: Margarita and Mexican meal; musical decor; food to melt in the mouth.

Discount Dining
Look for discount dining coupons in the myriad of brochures, flyers and tourist magazines. You'll find them in hotel lobbies, visitor information centers and just about everywhere tourists are found.

Fun Fact
It would take you nearly five years to eat in Orlando's 5,390 restaurants, if you ate in three each day.

paellas and cazuelas. Many of the ingredients are imported from Spain, as are the excellent wines. A central tapas bar, tiled pillars, high ceilings, and live flamenco entertainment make for a great atmosphere.

HUE Restaurant

629 E. Central Boulevard; tel: 407-849-1800; www.huerestaurant.com; Sun-Wed 11.30am–11pm, Thur–Sat 11.30am–midnight, Sun brunch 11am–4pm; $$–$$$

This trendy urban bistro is one of the hottest places in town. The bar has a popular happy hour – the outdoor tables on the corner terrace are great for people-watching. The restaurant features high-style yet relaxing urban design and a menu of progressive American cuisine, with wood-grilled meat, salmon and swordfish dishes and Asian flavors.

International Drive

Café Tu Tu Tango

8625 International Drive; tel: 407-248-2222; www.cafetututango. com/orlando; daily for lunch and dinner; $

Part of a funky restaurant chain with bohemian decor designed to resemble

---

Price guide for a two-course dinner for one with half a bottle of house wine, not including tax and tip:

$$$	above US$50
$$	US$25–50
$	below US$25

---

an artist's garret in Barcelona. The food is an array of international tapas-style dishes meant to be shared. Local artists paint, sculpt or perform in exchange for food and their art is for sale in the restaurant.

A Land Remembered

9939 Universal Boulevard at the Rosen Shingle Creek; tel: 407-996-3663; www.landremembered restaurant.com; daily 5.30–10pm; $$$

Named after Patrick Smith's novel, this classic steakhouse is decorated with photographs and artifacts from Florida's past. It features natural prime Black Angus beef from the Harris Ranch, as well as seafood and other fish dishes. Fine dining and excellent service.

Seasons 52

Plaza Venezia, 7700 Sand Lake Road; tel: 407-354-5212; www.seasons52. com; Mon–Fri 11.30am–2.30pm, 5–10pm (11pm Fri); Sat 11.30am–11pm, Sun 11.30am–10pm; $$

The focus here on fresh seasonal foods, natural cooking techniques, healthy, low calorie meals and creative dishes, all served in an appealing atmosphere, makes this place a winner. The 'mini-indulgences' – small-size desserts – even let you satisfy your sweet tooth guilt-free. Long international wine list with 70 wines served by the glass.

Sharks Underwater Grill

SeaWorld, 7007 SeaWorld Drive; tel: 407/351-3600 or 1-800-327-2424; daily 11am–park closing; $$–$$$

Set beside the enormous Sharks Encounter aquarium: one entire wall of the Underwater Grill's dining room is exposed to the tank, letting you sit in awe of the magnificent creatures swimming past. The food here, mostly seafood, is exquisite; the restaurant can easily produce one of the best meals you'll have at a theme park.

Tommy Bahama's Tropical Café

9101 International Drive at Pointe Orlando; tel: 321-281-5888; www. tommybahama.com; Sun–Thur 11am–11pm, Fri–Sat 11am–midnight; $$$

This island-style bar and restaurant is a brilliant accessory to the popular clothing store chain. There's a big outdoor terrace while inside the dark-wood bar and comfy booths lend a casual-chic atmosphere. Vegetables are not an afterthought here, with plump asparagus spears and other delights rounding out a superb menu of seafood and Caribbean influenced dishes, from coconut shrimp to the pork chops marinated in maple syrup.

Kissimmee and Celebration

Bruno's Italian Restaurant

8556 W. Highway 192, Kissimmee; tel: 407-397-7577; daily 11.30am–11pm; $–$$

Friendly Italian restaurant, popular with locals and visitors who find it tucked away beside the 7-Eleven on the south side of the road. There's a good selection of seafood pastas, veal and chicken entrées alongside interesting pizzas and pastas.

Columbia Restaurant

649 Front Street, downtown Celebration, tel: 407-566-1505; www.columbiarestaurant.com; daily 11.30am–10.30pm; $$–$$$

The Orlando branch of this century-old family-run restaurant *(see Tampa p.123)* overlooks the lake and serves delicious Spanish-Cuban cuisine. It also has an outdoor café and tapas bar.

Kenzie's Steak House

Mystic Dunes Golf Club, Old Lake Wilson Road, 1 mile south of Hwy 192; tel: 407-787-5646; lunch and dinner daily; $$–$$$

It's worth going off the beaten track to find this pleasant, casual restaurant, located in the midst of the Mystic Dunes Golf Resort overlooking the 18th green. It's a favorite with the locals for its excellent steaks and seafood dishes. Eat in the large dining room or outdoors on the patio terrace.

New York Pizza World

7531 W. Hwy 192, Kissimmee; tel: 407-390-9664; daily 11am–11pm; $

Cheap and cheerful Italian restaurant, a good alternative to the chains along this busy tourist stretch. Excellent pizzas and lasagne, calzones and pasta dishes. But give the house wine a miss.

Terrace Grille

Lakeland Terrace Hotel, 329 E. Main Street, Lakeland; tel: 863-688-0800; www.terracehotel.com; 11.30am–2.30pm, 5–10pm; $$$

With its tall arched windows and paneled high ceiling, the elegant restaurant

Above from far left: the healthy option; seafood creation, piled high; pretty pizza.

Lunchtime Bargains

If your budget won't stretch to the high-end gourmet restaurants, see if they are open at lunchtime. You'll often find many of the same chef-inspired dishes on the menu, in equal portions at a much lower price.

of the Lakeland Terrace hotel takes you back to the glamour of the 1920s. Highly acclaimed as one of Central Florida's best restaurants, the menu of New American cuisine features such well thought-out dishes as porcini dusted sea bass with roasted red pepper mashed potatoes, and grilled venison tenderloin with sweet potato gratin. The puddings are sublime too.

310 Park South

310 Park Avenue S, Winter Park; tel: 407-647-7277; www.310park-south.net; Mon–Wed 11am–10pm, Thur–Sat 11am–11pm, Sun 10am–10pm; $$–$$$

Large, buzzing restaurant with casual café-style seating and sidewalk tables. There are a range of sandwiches and salads for light meals, entrées feature continental cuisine. Good wine list with over 40 wines served by the glass. Late night menu till midnight Tues–Sat, Sunday brunch 10am–2pm.

Café de France

526 Park Avenue South, Winter Park; tel: 407-647-1869; www.lecafede france.com; Tue–Sat 11.30am–2.30pm, 6–10pm; $$–$$$

Price guide for a two-course dinner for one with half a bottle of house wine, not including tax and tip:

$$$	above US$50
$$	US$25–50
$	below US$25

With native French owners, you can be sure the menu includes authentic, traditional fare. Start your meal with foie gras, escargots or the daily selection of pâté before enjoying a fine selection of soups and salads and entrées that include lamb, pork, and a fish of the day. There's also a fine wine list of international vintages.

Luma on Park

290 S. Park Avenue, Winter Park; tel: 407-599-4111; www.lumaonpark. com; Mon–Thur 5.30–10pm, Fri and Sat 5.30–11pm, Sun 5.30–9pm, lounge opens from 4pm daily; $$$

This is perhaps the finest dining experience in the buzzing Park Avenue restaurant scene, with ultra-modern decor and creative dishes prepared in the open kitchen. Seafood features heavily on the menu, from scallops to barramundi, and there are steaks and chops, too. The wine list consists of boutique winemakers, mostly from California, and uniquely, half-glasses are available for those who would like to change wines for each course yet remain upright.

Park Plaza Gardens

319 Park Avenue South, Winter Park; tel: 407-645-2475; www.park plazagardens.com; Mon–Sat 11am–2.30pm and Sun–Mon 6–9pm, Tue–Sat 6-10pm, Sun brunch 11am–3pm; $$$

Adjoining the Park Plaza Hotel, the beautiful dining room is set in an enclosed brick courtyard with tropical plants and trees under the glass roof.

There's also a hip café with a bar and outdoor tables which keeps longer hours. The setting complements perfectly the top-rated gourmet menu featuring New American cuisine, with dishes such as coriander-crusted pork tenderloin and crab-stuffed grouper.

The Space Coast

Shark Pit Bar & Grill

4001 N. Atlantic Avenue, Cocoa Beach; tel: 321-868-8957; www.cocoabeachsurf.com; daily 6.30am–11pm; $$

Adjoining the Sheraton Four Points Hotel and part of the Cocoa Beach Surf Company, this laid-back restaurant and lounge lets you dine beside a 5,600-gallon aquarium that is home to sharks and exotic fish. The menu is relaxed too, with a tasty range of salads, sandwiches, seafood and grilled meat entrées, and great brick-oven pizzas.

The Surf

2 S. Atlantic Avenue at Minuteman Causeway, Cocoa Beach; tel: 321-783-2401; Sun–Thur 11am–10pm, Fri–Sat 11am–11pm; $$–$$$

You can't go wrong here, with three restaurants in one: a fine dining room featuring specialty fish dishes and steak house entrées; a casual bar and grill, also strong on seafood but with lighter entrées such as the fantastic fish tacos; and Shuckleberry Fin's Oyster Bar. Daily specials and happy hours make this relaxed spot even more of a local favorite.

Tampa Bay

Bern's Steakhouse

1208 S. Howard Avenue, Tampa; tel: 813-251-2421; www.bernssteak house.com; Sun–Thur 5–10pm, Fri–Sat 5–11pm; $$$

The late Bern Laxer's passion for fine steak and fine wines is elevated to an art at his namesake restaurant. Here perfectly aged steaks are hand-cut to order and expertly cooked to your liking. To accompany them, choose from one of the world's largest wine cellars, with 6,500 bottles. Service is impeccable, and after dinner your waiter will take you on a tour of the kitchen, where everything is homemade including the cheeses, and the amazing wine cellar. Then indulge some more in the decadent and intimate Harry Waugh Dessert Room upstairs.

Columbia Restaurant

2117 E. 7th Avenue, Ybor City, Tampa; tel: 813-248-4961; www.columbiarestaurant.com; Mon–Thu 11am–10pm, Fri–Sat 11am–11pm, Sun noon–9pm; $$

Founded in 1905 as a corner café for Ybor City's Cuban immigrants, the Columbia is Florida's oldest restaurant. Today its beautifully tiled facade extends along an entire block and contains 15 dining rooms. The delicious, award-winning Spanish-Cuban cuisine includes such favorites as snapper Alicante, roast pork à la Cubana, and paella. Be sure to book ahead if you want to dine during one of the two nightly flamenco dance performances (small cover charge).

Above from far left: poached fillet of sole; ocean-fresh oysters; lunch in Columbia Restaurant.

Mealtimes
American meal times are earlier than in Europe. Most restaurants open for lunch around 11 or 11.30am and serve til around 2.30pm; some in busy tourist areas stay open throughout the day. Dinner hours are generally from 5 or 5.30pm until 10 or 11pm. Waits of an hour or more are commonplace in high-traffic areas like the restaurants along Highway 192, so don't wait until you're starving to find a restaurant. Make a reservation if possible, or come early or late.

CREDITS

Insight Step by Step Orlando
Written by: Donna Dailey
Edited by: Carine Tracanelli
Series Editor: Clare Peel
Cartography Editors: Zoë Goodwin and James Macdonald
Picture Manager: Steven Lawrence
Art Editor: Ian Spick
Production: Kenneth Chan
Photography by: 4Corners Images 30-1, 30-2, 98; AA World Travel Library/TopFoto 57-2; Busch Entertainment Corporation 55-2; Ian Dagnall/Alamy 59-1, 62-4; Donna Dailey 2-5, 7-5, 19 (all), 22-3, 59-3, 60-1, 62-2, 62-3, 64-1, 66-1, 66-2, 67-2, 68-1, 69-2, 71-2, 72, 73 (all), 76-1, 76-2, 76-3, 77 (all), 82 (all), 83-1, 83-2, 84-2, 85-2, 94-2, 117 (all); Disney 2-7, 6-3, 12-1, 12-2, 13-1, 22-6, 24-1, 24-2, 26-1, 26-2, 26-4, 27, 28-1, 28-2, 29-2, 29-3, 31, 32 (all), 33-2, 33-3, 34 (all), 35-1, 36-2, 37-2, 39 (all), 40 (all), 41-2, 42 (all), 43 (all), 110, 111; Everett Collection 38-2; Jane Faircloth/Transparencies Inc. 55-1; Dave B. Fleetham/Tom Stack & Associates 30-3; Allan Friedlander/SuperStock 22-1; Patrick Frilet/ hemis.fr 56-2; Todd Gipstein/Corbis 35-1; Glo Lounge 17-1; Claire Griffiths 25, 38-1, 89-1; Hard Rock Hotel Orlando 112-2; Blaine Harrington III/Corbis 2-1; Charles Hosmer Morse Museum of American Art 2-3, 6-2, 78-1, 78-2, 78-4, 79 (all); James Houck/Alamy 56-1; I Ride 107-2; iStockphoto.com 6-1, 8-2, 15-3, 33-1, 52-1, 59-2, 63-3, 96-1, 118 (all), 122-1; Britta Jaschinski/APA 120-1, 121; JJM Stock Photography/Florida/Alamy 61; Norman Kelly/fotoLibra 8-1; The Kennedy Space Center 7-1, 22-2, 86-1, 87, 88-2; James Lemass 44-3, 53-2, 56-4; Leonardo 112-1; Library of Congress 20-2, 20-3, 26-3; Mennello Museum of American Folk Art 64-2; Richard Nowitz/APA 2-2, 2-4, 4 (all), 6-4, 6-5, 7-2, 7-3, 7-4, 8-3, 8-4, 8-5, 8-6, 8-7, 10 (all), 11-1, 11-2, 12-4, 13-2, 13-3, 14-1, 14-2, 14-3, 15-1, 15-2, 16 (all), 17-2, 18-2, 22-4, 22-7, 44-1, 44-2, 46-2, 49-1, 51-2, 53-1, 54 (all), 56-3, 60-2, 65-1, 74 (all), 75-2, 75-3, 76-4, 83-3, 84-1, 85-1, 86-2, 86-3, 88-1, 89-2, 89-3, 90, 91, 92 (all), 93 (all), 94-1, 94-3, 94-4, 95 (all), 96-2, 96-3, 96-4, 96-5, 96-6, 97-7, 99, 100 (all), 101 (all), 102-2, 103 (all), 104 (all), 106 (all), 108, 109, 114 (all), 115, 116 (all), 119, 120-2, 122-2, 123; Timothy O'Keefe 22-5, 48-2, 49-2, 49-3, 50-2, 51-1, 68-2; Timothy O'Keefe/Alamy 58-1, 62-1; Orange County Regional History Center 20-1, 21; Orlando Museum of Art 65-2, 65-3, 65-4; Orlando/Orange County Convention & Visitors Bureau Inc 14-4, 29-1, 57-1, 78-3, 80-2, 81; Rough Guides/Alamy 58-2, 80-1; John Taylor/Alamy 70-2; Tebeau-Field Library of Florida History 11-3; Universal Orlando Resort 46-3, 48-3; Wet 'n Wild 70-4, 71-1; Art Wolfe 41-1; Gregory Wrona/Apa 2-7, 12-3, 18-1, 28-3, 35-2, 36-3, 37-1, 45 (all), 46-1, 47 (all), 48-1, 50-1, 50-3, 52-2, 53-3, 53-4, 63-1, 63-2, 66-3, 67-1, 68-3, 69-1, 70-1, 70-3, 75-1, 102-1, 105, 107-1, 113.

Cover: main image: ICIMAGE/Alamy; bottom left: iStockphoto.com; bottom right: Purestock/SuperStock.

Printed by: Insight Print Services (Pte) Ltd, 38 Joo Koon Road, Singapore 628990

© 2008 Apa Publications GmbH & Co. Verlag KG (Singapore branch)

All rights reserved

First Edition 2008

No part of this book may be reproduced, stored in a retrieval system or transmitted in any form or by any means (electronic, mechanical, photocopying, recording or otherwise), without prior written permission of Apa Publications. Brief text quotations with use of photographs are exempted for book review purposes only. Information has been obtained from sources believed to be reliable, but its accuracy and completeness, and the opinions based thereon, are not guaranteed.

www.insightguides.com

DISTRIBUTION

WORLDWIDE

Apa Publications GmbH & Co. Verlag KG (Singapore branch), 38 Joo Koon Road, Singapore 628990
Tel: (65) 6865 1600
Fax: (65) 6861 6438

UK AND IRELAND

GeoCenter International Ltd
Meridian House, Churchill Way West, Basingstoke, Hampshire, RG21 6YR
Tel: (44) 01256 817 987
Fax: (44) 01256 817 988

UNITED STATES

Langenscheidt Publishers, Inc.
36–36 33rd Street, 4th Floor, Long Island City, NY 11106
Tel: (1) 718 784 0055
Fax: (1) 718 784 0640

AUSTRALIA

Universal Publishers
1 Waterloo Road, Macquarie Park, NSW 2113
Tel: (61) 2 9857 3700
Fax: (61) 2 9888 9074

NEW ZEALAND

Hema Maps New Zealand Ltd (HNZ)
Unit D, 24 Ra ORA Drive, East Tamaki, Auckland
Tel: (64) 9 273 6459
Fax: (64) 9 273 6479

CONTACTING THE EDITORS

We would appreciate it if readers would alert us to errors or outdated information by writing to us at insight@apaguide.co.uk or Apa Publications, PO Box 7910, London SE1 1WE, UK.

INDEX